PRAYER 365

MICHAEL L. RUFFIN

To Linda + Kenneth —

With much admiration &
appreciation!

Michael L. Ruffin

Published in the United States by Nurturing Faith Inc., Macon GA,
www.nurturingfaith.net.

Library of Congress Cataloging-in-Publication Data is available.

ISBN 978-1-938514-03-6

CONTENTS

To Debra,
my partner in life and in prayer,
to whom my heart was drawn the first time I heard her pray,
and whose prayers have sustained me for more than three decades

INTRODUCTION

At the end of 2009, I adopted a discipline of writing a prayer every day. This book is a collection of a year's worth of those prayers.

Prayer is, on the one hand, a personal matter. There is no one "correct" way to pray, so this offering of prayers is not meant to offer a model of how to pray. These prayers come out of my experience, out of my life, and out of my pilgrimage. I share them with the hope that they will somehow connect with your life as many friends have affirmed they have connected with theirs. Hopefully there is enough commonality in human experience that my prayers will prove helpful in leading you to pray as you need to pray and in the way you pray best.

Prayer is, on the other hand, a communal matter. Jesus did, after all, teach us to pray to "Our Father" and not to "My Father." One reason I love praying the Lord's Prayer or the Psalms or other ancient prayers in a worship service is that not only are all of us who are gathered in that place praying together, but we are also praying with many others who are praying those prayers. Indeed we are praying with all those who have gone before us and who will come after us. Such praying connects us with the communion of saints. Perhaps, in a small way, those who choose to pray the prayers in this book will find in the knowledge that others are praying them, too, a meaningfully enlarged sense of Christian community. I hope so.

A word is in order regarding the organization of the prayers in this volume. The prayers are divided into sections by days of the week. The book begins with 52 prayers for Sunday, then moves to 52 prayers for Monday, and so on through the final section that contains 52 prayers for Saturday. So, you can begin using the prayers at any time during the year. If you begin at some other time than the beginning of the calendar year, though, you should be aware that certain prayers are somewhat seasonal in nature. Therefore, it would be best to begin reading at the place in the year corresponding to the point in the year when you begin reading. In other words, if you begin using the prayers in the book on the Sunday of the 26th week of the year, begin with Sunday 26, then go to Monday 26, then Tuesday 26, and so on. When you arrive at Saturday 25, you will have gone all the way through the prayers.

While the book is not arranged according to the Christian year, some note is made of it. The prayers for Friday 51 and Saturday 51 are Holy Week prayers, respectively. If you choose to read these prayers on the holy days in a year in which these holy days do not correspond to the days as numbered in this volume, some simple swapping will allow you still to have a prayer to read for each day.

Michael L. Ruffin
Season of Lent, 2012

Sunday Prayers

- SUNDAY 1 -
The Lord's Day

Remind us that

the Wise Men thought they were coming to worship the son of Herod but instead they found the Son of God, the Son of Man, the Son of Mary,

the One born to bring down the powerful from their thrones and to lift up the lowly, to fill the hungry with good things and to send the rich away empty.

Cause us to worship that One today and all days—
not the son of Herod.

Cause us to be the sisters and brothers of that one today and all days—
not of the son of Herod.

Amen.

- SUNDAY 2 -
The Lord's Day

O God,

on this Lord's Day,
this Resurrection Day,
this "Little Easter" Day,

turn our full attention to the facts that Jesus Christ is risen from the dead and we have been raised to new life in him and we will be raised from the dead.

Cause us to practice, to rehearse these great truths on this Sunday so that on

Monday,
Tuesday,
Wednesday,
Thursday,
Friday,
Saturday,

we will remember them so as to live in light of them.

Amen.

- SUNDAY 3 -
The Lord's Day

O Lord,

every day is your day; but today is especially your day, for it is

the day you rose from the dead,
the day you conquered death,
the day you gave us life.

Cause us on this Lord's Day—

like the women who discovered it at dawn,
like the two who discovered it after a sprint to the tomb,
like the two who discovered it after an afternoon stroll,
like the one who said I don't believe it,
like the gang huddled together like we will be today—

to feel the wonder,
to embrace the mystery,
to fight through the doubt,
to see the possibilities,
to live the life that must be ours

because Christ is risen indeed.

Amen.

- SUNDAY 4-
The Lord's Day

On this Lord's Day,

may we lift up our eyes to look to the One who was lifted up on the cross;
may we offer up our lives to the One who offered up his life for us;
may we give up ourselves for the sake of the One who gave himself up for God's sake and for our sake;
may we take up our crosses in obedience to the One who took up his cross;
may we raise up our hearts and voices and lives in praise of the One who was raised from the dead.

Amen.

- SUNDAY 5 -

The Lord's Day

We are in your presence every day, O Lord, but on the Lord's Day—on Sunday, when we "go to church"—we imagine ourselves especially coming into your presence, which I suppose we are.

In your presence there is comfort. Would you today comfort those who will come into your presence depressed, grieving, anxious, hopeless, confused, or lonely?

But—and we don't think about this enough—in your presence there is also danger, for you are, after all, God! And we are, after all, us.

It is dangerous to parade our sins arrogantly before you—our pride, our prejudices, our hate, and our self-righteousness.

So—

Forgive us. Break us.

It is also dangerous to bring our openness humbly before you—our willingness, our commitment, our brokenness, and our love.

Still—

Call us. Use us.

Lord, we are in danger either way. Please work in us so that we will be in the danger that makes the difference—the danger that comes from following Jesus in service and in sacrifice.

Not our will but thy will be done.

Amen.

- SUNDAY 6 -

The Lord's Day

The living of life can take its toll; the events of life can knock us about, leaving us bruised and bloodied and sometimes even defeated—as if the very life has been beaten out of us.

But then comes Sunday—the Lord's Day, Resurrection Day—to bring us back to life through the same life-giving power that brought Jesus back to life.

Thank you, God, for this Lord's Day and for the new life it will bring to us not only that we might live on that day but also for the living of these days.

Amen.

- SUNDAY 7 -

The Lord's Day

On that Sunday morning so long ago, the women went to the tomb expecting to find what one finds at a tomb—death, which is for lots of people another way of saying "nothing." The men who had followed Jesus didn't go at all, so maybe they figured there was less than nothing there to be found.

Much to their surprise—the women who were there first and the men who trailed along later to check out what the women had told them—

they found resurrection;

they found life.

On this Sunday morning—today—some of us will go to the church building and—forgive us, Lord—we may go expecting to find nothing or we may go expecting to find something, but thinking we already know what it is we will find. Some of us will not go at all because—forgive us, Lord—we figure that what we would find there is less than nothing, that it doesn't matter in the least.

Much to our surprise, Lord, whether we are those who plan to go expecting to find nothing or those who plan to stay figuring there is less than nothing going on there, let us find resurrection.

Let us find life.

On this Lord's Day, O God, surprise us!

Amen.

- SUNDAY 8 -
The Lord's Day

O Lord,

We live too much of our lives with

eyes screwed shut,
hands clenched tight,
minds closed off,
hearts locked up

like tombs sealed with a stone.

On this Lord's Day may

our eyes,
our hands,
our minds,
our hearts

be opened

like,
because of,
and
through

the one for whom, on that Sunday long ago,
the stone that sealed the tomb was rolled away.

Amen.

- SUNDAY 9 -
The Lord's Day

O God,

As your servant Paul taught us, "There is but one God, the Father from whom all things came and for whom we live; and there is but one Lord, Jesus Christ, through whom all things came and through whom we live" (1 Cor. 8:6). Without you, nothing was made that was made; without you, no life can be lived that is lived; without you, the thought of eternal life is but a fleeting wish. But with you, all things are and all things are possible.

Because you are God, we acknowledge that we can know you only because you desire to be known and that we can love you only because you desire to be loved.

Direct our full-hearted praise to you, inspired and magnified by our realization that it is not only by grace we are saved, but it is also by grace that we can know of you at all. How gracious you are to love us and to allow us to love you.

Remind us how amazing it is that when you think of us, you think of loving us and caring for us and being with us. Fill our hearts with thanksgiving over your loving-kindness and your mercy. Empower us to trust you with all of our hurts, with all of our fears, and with all of our needs.

Amen.

- SUNDAY 10 -
The Lord's Day

On this Lord's Day, O God, as we celebrate the resurrection of our Lord, we will do so in communion

with all those in the room with us;
with all those gathered in their places all over the world;
with all those who have gone before us;
with all the angels in heaven;
with the Father, Son, and Holy Spirit.

Thank you, Lord, for this blessed communion.
Thank you, Lord, for this reminder that we are not alone.

Amen.

- SUNDAY 11 -

The Lord's Day

Every day is a new day, a day we've never had before—but it's still a day. So while each day is in a sense familiar because there is a rhythm of the regular to it, each one is also full of difference and change because there is the eruption of the irregular in it.

Today is the Lord's Day, the day when we remember and celebrate what happened on that long-ago regular day, that Sunday when, like on all other Sundays back then, the regular and expected happened—the work week began and meals were eaten and greetings were shared and gain was rejoiced over and loss was grieved over—but also when something very irregular and unexpected happened that changed and has continued to change everything.

O God, on this Lord's Day we will share in the regularity of worship, the usual ways in which we remember and celebrate what happened on that first Lord's Day.

Cause us, though, to be open

to the irregular and the unexpected,
to whatever you want to say and do to us,
to however you want to change us,

through Jesus Christ our crucified and resurrected Lord.

Amen.

- SUNDAY 12 -

The Lord's Day

It is about response, this worship of ours. We praise you in response to who you are and in response to what you have done, are doing, and will do.

Then, empowered by that worship, we go back out into the world to continue our worship through our response to the world's need in response to your call.

So on this Lord's Day, O God, would you put us solidly in response mode, so that in our worship we might praise you and be inspired to serve you by serving others.

Amen.

- SUNDAY 13 -
The Lord's Day

There is something about singing.

One of the things about singing is that it releases what is inside us, be it good or bad, happy or sad—whether it be praise or lament or confession or petition.

In our worship on this Lord's Day we will sing. May we sing with integrity, honestly and openly and vulnerably, opening up our lives to you and pouring out whatever is inside us.

O God, may the pouring out in song of what is inside us be symbolic of—and a part of—the daily and constant pouring out of our lives in gratitude for you and in service to you.

Amen.

- SUNDAY 14 (OR PALM SUNDAY) -
The Lord's Day

On that first Palm Sunday so long ago, the followers of Jesus spread their cloaks and laid palm branches on the road so that the donkey on which Jesus rode could walk on them.

It was a tribute; it was a way to praise Jesus; it was a way to give something to him.

When it was over, I suppose they left the branches Jesus had walked over just lying there.

Help us, Lord, to learn to leave those things in our lives lying there that we need to leave lying there—our fears, our prejudices, our greed, our envy, our lusts, our selfishness, our anxieties, our sins—so that we might be less encumbered by them.

When it was over, I suppose they retrieved the cloaks Jesus had walked over and simply put them back on.

Help us, Lord, to learn to put those things back on that we need to put back on —our love, our service, our sacrifice, our gifts, our abilities, our time, our very lives—so that we might, having given them up, find them again.

We lay everything before you in praise to you today, Lord. Help us to leave there what needs to be left and to pick back up what needs to be picked up.

Amen.

- SUNDAY 15 (OR EASTER SUNDAY) -
The Lord's Day

Their souls were as empty as his tomb when the followers of Jesus got there that morning, but real soon their souls were full of him—
and that made all the difference.

O God, make us so empty of ourselves that we can be filled with the life of the resurrected Jesus—
because that will make all the difference.

Amen.

- SUNDAY 16 -
The Lord's Day

God is God whether we acknowledge God or not.
God is worthy whether we worship God or not.

So in some ways worship changes nothing.

But in some other ways worship changes everything because it makes a difference in us—in the ways we think, in the ways we decide, in the ways we choose, in the ways we act, and in the ways we relate.

God is God whether we worship God or not.
But we are not fully us if we don't.

Thank you, O God, for this Lord's Day when we gather to worship you. We acknowledge that our worship is all about you. Help us to embrace the change that comes to us as we do it.

Amen.

- SUNDAY 17 -
The Lord's Day

As we come before you on this Lord's Day—

our hats in our hands,
our hearts on our sleeves,
a lump in our throats,
a hole in our souls,
our lives on the line—

we come to worship you.

But first we have to find you.

You are there; it is our stuff that blocks our view. But what can we do? After all, we must bring ourselves before you, and our stuff comes with us—indeed, it goes with us wherever we go.

So Lord, would you clear the way? Would you clear our vision so that we can today truly worship you?

Amen.

- SUNDAY 18 -
The Lord's Day

There is a great Sunday coming, a great Easter, a great Resurrection Day, when all the dead in Christ will rise and so we will forever be with the One who rose before us to pave the way for us.

That is good to know as we live in and through those parts of our lives that are, in a sense, the days of our "little deaths," those events in which we are taken down into the pit, those events in which we sense the loss of life—or at least some part of our life.

We don't flee from those things. Such is life sometimes, and it is our calling to embrace it all, to learn from it all, to experience you in it all, to find and to share grace in it all, and to serve you and others in it all.

But Lord, how we need Sunday; how we need the Lord's Day; how we need a little resurrection in our lives.

So thank you for this Lord's Day. Thank you for the reminder of the resurrection of Jesus that was, of his resurrection power that is, and of our resurrection that will be.

Amen.

- SUNDAY 19 -
The Lord's Day

As we gather to worship today, O Lord, we gather also to practice the practices we need to carry out every day, every moment, of our lives.

We will practice focusing our attention on you.
We will practice reflecting on your love for us.
We will practice listening to you.
We will practice seeking your call in and your claim on our lives.
We will practice trusting in you.
We will practice depending on you.
We will practice sensing the presence of the Holy Spirit.
We will practice remembering our responsibilities to you, to the people around us, and to the world in which we live.
We will practice living in light of the reality of eternity and of the fact that you are working your purposes out even through our lives.
We will practice being with you in prayer.
We will practice singing praises to you.
We will practice giving ourselves to you.
We will practice being formed by your Word.
We will practice being your children.
We will practice following the crucified and resurrected Lord Jesus Christ.

On this Lord's Day, O God, help us to practice well the practices that will stand us in good stead on every day of the week.

Amen.

- SUNDAY 20 -

The Lord's Day

On this Lord's Day may we worship you, O God, in spirit and in truth.

May we, insofar as we can by your grace, your spirit, and the revelation through your Son Jesus Christ, know and worship you as you are.

May we worship you out of as complete an awareness as possible of who we are.

On this Lord's Day may we worship you, O God, in spirit and in truth.

Amen.

- SUNDAY 21 -

The Lord's Day

In worship on this Lord's Day we might

sit,
stand,
kneel,
bow,
listen,
read,
watch, or
speak.

Help us, Lord, not to go through the motions but rather to live into them so that we might with our bodies and our spirits—with everything we are—worship you.

Amen.

- SUNDAY 22 -

The Lord's Day

We worship on Sunday because it is the Lord's Day, the day Jesus Christ rose from the dead. But it is God in God's fullness—God as Holy Trinity; God as Father, Son, and Holy Spirit; God as Creator, Redeemer, and Sustainer—to whom our worship is directed.

O God, may our worship today be filled with

awe in the face of your magnificence,
wonder in the face of your majesty,
gratitude in the face of your grace,
challenge in the face of your holiness.

Amen.

- SUNDAY 23 -

The Lord's Day

Among many other things, resurrection means

despair giving way to joy,
the used-up giving way to the useful,
hope giving way to fulfillment,
longing giving way to consummation,
death giving way to life.

O God, on this Lord's Day, this day when we celebrate the resurrection of Jesus Christ, when we anticipate our future resurrection, and when we practice the presence of resurrection in our lives right here and right now, cause us who despair, who are used up, who hope, who long, and who are dying to experience instead joy, usefulness, fulfillment, consummation, and life.

Amen.

- SUNDAY 24 -
The Lord's Day

O God,

On this Lord's Day we come before you

seeking you,
responding to you,
needing you,
believing in you.

Or perhaps, even as we come before you, we may be

hiding from you,
running from you,
avoiding you,
doubting you.

As we come before you today, Lord, cause us to be not so certain of your presence that we cannot be surprised or not so intent on our absence that we will not be challenged.

Amen.

- SUNDAY 25 -
The Lord's Day

Early on a Sunday morning many years ago it seemed to a certain man's family and friends—as it has seemed to the family and friends of so many people on so many days before that Sunday and since that Sunday—that death had won.

But when some of that certain man's friends arrived at his grave early on that Sunday morning to pay their respects, they found a remarkable thing: he had left the grave!

And, to make the remarkable thing even more remarkable, he appeared to and spoke with and even ate with many of them over the next few weeks.

And, to make the remarkable thing yet more remarkable, it has been the experience of countless numbers of people since then that the man who was alive then dead then alive again has somehow been made real to them so that, through life and at the end of life, death does not for them have the final word.

O God, on this Lord's Day, the day on which we weekly celebrate the resurrection of our Lord Jesus Christ, cause us to know his presence with us and empower us through him to celebrate the victory of life over death that is ours because of him.

And God, please especially touch those who are grieving today because someone they love has died or is in the process of dying. Make the reality of resurrection as obvious to them as the breath they are breathing.

Amen.

- SUNDAY 26 -
The Lord's Day

Our worship of God is service to God. So in our worship on this Lord's Day help us, O God,

to offer ourselves to you,
to give our lives to you,
to submit ourselves to you.

Then, having done all that in the sanctuary, help us to go out into the world and to serve you there

by serving others,
by offering ourselves to them,
by giving our lives to them,
by submitting ourselves to them.

May our worship—our service—be an all-the-time practice.

Amen.

- SUNDAY 27 -
The Lord's Day

"This is the day the Lord has made; we will rejoice and be glad in it." Of all the days the Lord has made, Sunday is the best because in God's grace what happened one Sunday is what has made, does make, and will make all the difference.

For it was on a Sunday that the Lord Jesus Christ rose from the dead, thereby giving us hope—assurance—of eternal life, of real life, of life full of life.

On this Sunday, this Lord's Day, how can we do other than praise you for all you accomplished in the resurrection of your Son?

May our praise today be grounded in the resurrection of our Lord, and when we leave our place of worship may our lives be grounded in that same reality.

Amen.

- SUNDAY 28 -
The Lord's Day

Different ones of us will enter the place of worship today in different ways.

Some of us will walk in with no sense that such walking is any different an act than walking into the grocery store or the restaurant or the barbershop.

Some of us will saunter in despite our sins or perhaps in denial of them, bearing little awareness or acceptance of our need to repent.

Some of us will drag in, head down, ashamed, unable or unwilling to allow ourselves to be enveloped in the grace and forgiveness the Lord has given us.

O God, regardless of how we walk into the place of worship today, please do something to us and with us once we are there.

Cause us to experience awe in the presence of Almighty God.

Cause us to experience grace in the presence of the Lord Jesus Christ who died and rose again so that we might have eternal life.

Cause us to experience empowerment in the presence of the Holy Spirit.

However we walk in, O God, grant us an experience of worship that will result in our walking out different—better—than we were when we entered.

Amen.

- SUNDAY 29 -
The Lord's Day

While there are many reasons, not all of them necessarily good ones, that we go to the church building to worship you on Sunday, the main reason is that we want to worship—to serve—the God who caused the crucified Jesus to rise from the grave on that Sunday morning so long ago.

Remind us today of that main reason, O God, and cause it to be uppermost in our minds as we worship today.

Remind us of the wonder and glory and presence of the resurrected Jesus in our worship today.

And then remind us of the wonder and glory and presence of the resurrected Jesus as we go out to live in the world this week.

After all, while Jesus was raised on a Sunday, since then he has been raised all the time!

In him, so are we and so will we be.

Thanks be to God!

Amen.

- SUNDAY 30 -
The Lord's Day

We will limp into worship today. We will enter the sanctuary bearing the marks of the struggles and the battles and the missteps of last week, of last month, of last year—of a lifetime.

There is a sense in which we find healing in your presence. Your forgiveness and grace and mercy go a long way, and we are thankful.

There is also a sense in which we are enabled by your grace to live with our limp, to embrace it, and to regard it as evidence of our progress and our growth and our service, particularly if we are enabled by your grace to see our struggles as struggles not only with other people and with ourselves but also with you.

There is also a sense in which, if we enter worship today strutting, it will be a good thing if we have an encounter with you that sends us away limping.

On this Lord's Day, bless our limps.
If necessary, give us another one.

Amen.

- SUNDAY 31 -
The Lord's Day

Various things connect those within a group to each other.

They might be connected, for example, by

a common interest,
a common ethnicity,
a common nationality,
a common language,
a common locality,
a common cause, or
a common enemy.

Truth be told, we who gather today to worship are bound by some of those same things, and that is not always to our credit—especially when one of those things is for us the main thing.

Remind us on this Lord's Day, O God, that what really connects us with those with whom we gather to worship is what connects us as well with all those who worship you everywhere—a common grace we have found in your Son Jesus Christ.

May that grace be by far the main reality that connects us with each other as we worship you today.

Amen.

- SUNDAY 32 -
The Lord's Day

Today many groups of people will gather as a body to worship.

As a part of their worship, many of those bodies of believers will share in the Lord's Supper, in the Eucharist, in Communion.

O God, as we receive the body of Christ, cause us to remember that his body was broken for us and that by his stripes we are healed. Cause us furthermore to remember his continuing presence with us.

And God, as we receive the body of Christ, cause us to remember that we who are the church are the body of Christ in the world today. Make us willing to be broken for the sake of the world. Make us willing to be present with the hurting and lost people of our communities.

"This is his body."
"We are his body."

Amen.

- SUNDAY 33 -
The Lord's Day

We bring it all before you in worship today:

our love and hate,
our mercy and anger,
our forgiveness and unforgiveness,
our trust and fear,
our faith and doubt,
our likes and dislikes,
our selflessness and selfishness,
our plenty and lack,
our health and sickness,
our faithfulness and faithlessness,
our comfort and unease,
our gladness and sorrow,
our life and death.

We lay it all on the altar before you on this Lord's Day.

Please accept our sacrifice even as we accept yours.

Amen.

- SUNDAY 34 -
The Lord's Day

The money we give is but a part of the offering we make in worship.

We also offer our attention, our triumphs, our wholeness, our defeats, our fears, our thoughts, our actions, our mistakes, our relationships, our time, our abilities, our love, our faith, our ignorance, our work, our knowledge, our service—we offer, in other words, our lives.

O Lord, we will offer you our lives in worship today; cause us to remember as we go out into the world that our offering continues.

Amen.

- SUNDAY 35 -
The Lord's Day

The women who went to the tomb early on that Sunday morning got quite a surprise; an empty tomb was hardly what they expected to find, not to mention a resurrected Jesus.

I wonder how quickly they got used to the idea.

Forgive us, Lord, for being so used to the idea that the resurrected Jesus goes with us that we give it—we give him—little thought and thus fail to open ourselves up to the possibilities created by his resurrection and by his presence.

O God, as we go to worship you on this Lord's Day, surprise us. Get our attention. Remind us of the real power of the resurrection.

And help us never to get used to it.

Amen.

- SUNDAY 36 -
The Lord's Day

O God,

As we come before you in worship today,
we are all on our way, even though

some of us are lost on our way;
some of us are wandering on our way;
some of us are searching on our way;
some of us are progressing on our way;
some of us are regressing on our way;
some of us are set in our ways.

Inspire us today to submit our way to the One who is the Way so that we might walk in his Way of love, grace, service, and sacrifice.

Amen.

- SUNDAY 37 -
The Lord's Day

O God,

Maybe it is not that whatever place we gather in to worship you today is more holy than any other place; after all, since you are everywhere and since you are holy, every place must also be holy.

Maybe it is rather that we need a place to go occasionally that seems a little holier than other places so that we can be reminded to look for the holiness everywhere—to look for you everywhere.

Also, the fact that we gather to worship on Sunday because that was the day the Lord Jesus Christ was raised from the dead does not mean Jesus is raised only on Sunday; no, Jesus is raised all the time.

So we gather today to worship you on the day our Lord was raised so that we will remember to live every day in the light of our knowledge of the presence of our resurrected Lord.

O God, we will enter our holy place today to worship you on the day Jesus was raised from the dead.

Empower us to exit that place with our eyes and spirits wide open to the holiness in the world and in our lives—because you are in the world and in our lives—and to the life and hope in the world and in our lives—because the resurrected Christ is in the world and in our lives.

Amen.

- SUNDAY 38 -
The Lord's Day

We have just finished a week of wandering, and now we are beginning another one.

Hopefully our wanderings have been and will be marked by a desire to follow you and to do your will, in which case we have been and will be aware—at least way down deep—that you are with us in our wandering and that in some mysterious way we are wandering with a purpose and toward a destination.

It may be, though, that we have been wandering more or less on our own, giving you no place and no thought, and so our wandering seems without purpose and without a goal. Even then, while we may not have a sense of you being with us in our wandering, the truth is that you in your great mercy are right behind us, pursuing us lovingly and relentlessly and fiercely.

Thank you, Lord.

On this Lord's Day, as our wanderings do or don't take us into a place of worship, cause us, as our particular kind of wandering gives us opportunity, to celebrate your presence with us or to turn around to find you in pursuit of us.

Amen.

- SUNDAY 39 -
The Lord's Day

On this Lord's Day we will gather to worship God who raised Jesus Christ from death.

We believe the resurrected Christ is among us.

But most of our worship will be based on and built around second-hand accounts, on testimony. That testimony will come in the form of Scripture, sermon, and songs.

O God, cause that testimony to touch our hearts, minds, and spirits and to inspire our turning to you, whether for the first time or in a new and necessary way.

Thank you that in your grace you use what we can see with our eyes and hear with our ears to turn us toward the resurrected One who can be experienced only through faith.

Amen.

- SUNDAY 40 -
The Lord's Day

Sunday is a day that plays a double role.

It is the first day of a new week.
It feels like the last day of the old week.

As such, Sunday offers an opportunity to reflect upon and to evaluate the old week and to look forward to and to pray over the new week.

Over all such Sunday reflections and evaluations, and over all such Sunday anticipation and prayer hangs the resurrection of our Lord Jesus Christ whom we remember and celebrate every Sunday.

O God, on this Sunday, thank you for those times last week when we lived in the power of the resurrection. Forgive us for where we failed to live in the power of the resurrection, and help us to view the possibilities and mysteries of the coming week through the lens of the resurrection.

On this Sunday—this Lord's Day, this Resurrection Day—inspire and empower us to see everything, be it past, present, or future, in the light of the reality of Jesus' resurrection, in the light of the fact he has been raised—and he is raised—and in the light of the fact we have been raised—and we will be raised.

Amen.

- SUNDAY 41 -
The Lord's Day

On this Lord's Day many churches will partake of the Lord's Supper. Some of us call it the Eucharist, which means thanksgiving.

So as we partake, O Lord, help us to do so with a great sense of thanksgiving for all Jesus Christ did for us in the giving of his body and in the shedding of his blood.

We thank you for

the forgiveness of sin,
the bestowal of grace,
the experience of love,
the defeat of death, and
the gift of eternal life

that are ours in our crucified and resurrected Lord Jesus Christ.

May our worship today be filled with thanksgiving.

Amen.

- SUNDAY 42 -
The Lord's Day

As we gather to worship you on this Lord's Day, O Lord, we may do so with the family of faith with whom we gather week after week, or we may do so with a family of faith nearby or far away with whom we worship occasionally, or we may do so with a family of faith with whom we have never gathered before and with whom we may never gather again.

Wherever we worship and with whomever we worship today, remind us we are all of us in a very real way together all the time; we are together in our serving of one Lord, in our exercise of one faith, and in our participation in one baptism.

Cause us to celebrate the fact that in Christ we worship and serve together, regardless of how far apart geographically and culturally and linguistically we may be.

Amen.

- SUNDAY 43 -

The Lord's Day

On this Lord's Day,

We will worship you who sits enthroned in the heavens.

Lord, we believe; help our unbelief.

We will celebrate the resurrection of your Son Jesus, who makes all the difference in our lives and in history.

Lord, we believe; help our unbelief.

We will contemplate the presence of and will seek the guidance of the Holy Spirit who is you with us.

Lord, we believe; help our unbelief.

We will commit ourselves to follow the way Jesus walked.

Lord, we believe; help our unbelief.

We will go back out into the world hoping to serve you a little more faithfully.

Lord, we believe; help our unbelief.

O God, we do not ask you to increase our certainty because increased certainty tends us toward arrogance.

We ask rather that you would increase our faith because increased faith tends us toward humble trust.

Amen.

- SUNDAY 44 -

The Lord's Day

The congregations gathering for worship today are of varying sizes. They range in size from one or two to many thousands—and the number doesn't really matter.

Cause us, Lord, to remember that whether our particular gathering is small or large or medium in number, we are all part of a spectacularly huge congregation—a congregation comprised of all of those in the world who are worshipping you plus all of those in heaven, both the heavenly hosts and the great host of saints who are with you now, who join in our worship.

Thank you, Lord, for your congregation of which we are privileged to be a part.

Amen.

- SUNDAY 45 -

The Lord's Day

We worship you because we love you, O God. May our worship of you on this Lord's Day be an appropriate display of our love; may it display

commitment,
joy,
passion,
curiosity,
wonder,
appreciation,
faithfulness, and
anticipation.

We love you, O God, and so we look forward to spending quality time with you in worship today.

Amen.

- SUNDAY 46 -

The Lord's Day

The experiences of our lives call forth response.

Sometimes that response is a blink of the eyes or a shrug of the shoulders.

Sometimes that response is logical and can be expressed prosaically; we can talk about it.

Sometimes, though, we don't know what to say or we can't quite put our response into words.

That's where the Spirit of God translates for us.
That's where music speaks for us.

Thank you, O God, that on this Lord's Day we can practice together what happens to us all every day—having experiences that call forth responses that can only be expressed spiritually and musically and lyrically.

Through today's prayers and through today's songs, teach us to let flow in and through us the language of Spirit and of music—even though it can't be "spoken"—that will enable us honestly and openly to express the deep pain and the deep joy our lives have buried in our hearts.

Amen.

- SUNDAY 47 -

The Lord's Day

It is not our place to crown Jesus king—Jesus *is* king.

He is king over creation.
He is king over the church.
He is king over us.
He is king over everything.

It is our place to acknowledge his kingship and to commit our lives more fully to serving him.

In his crucifixion and resurrection we see that Jesus is king over life and over death and over life after death.

May our worship of you today, O God, be a proper acknowledgement and celebration of the kingship of your Son Jesus Christ. May it be a true submission of every part of our lives to him—since he is king over every part of our lives, including the parts that are yet to come.

Amen.

- SUNDAY 48 -
The Lord's Day

We gather to worship on this Lord's Day because we need to celebrate hope fulfilled.

The Savior did come to our world all those years ago.
The Savior does come to our lives here and now.

In his coming hope is fulfilled.

We gather to worship on this Lord's Day because we need to anticipate the fulfillment of hope unfulfilled.

The Savior will come to our world some day. The Savior will make this broken creation and our incomplete lives whole some day.

In his coming, hope will be fulfilled.

Lord, we bring our hope with us to worship; we will take our hope with us back out into the world.

May our hope be characterized not by frustration that results from our thinking we know how it all should go, but rather by expectation that results from our knowledge that you know how it all should go.

Amen.

- SUNDAY 49 -

The Lord's Day

On this Lord's Day, O God, lead us to celebrate your love for us by celebrating your commitment to us, your faithfulness to us, and your ruthless pursuit of us—because biblically speaking, your love is your commitment, your faithfulness, and your pursuit.

The coming of Jesus is the epitome of that love. So as we anticipate his coming, help us to anticipate a more complete understanding of and reception of your love.

Cause us, O God, to respond to your commitment to us with our commitment to you, to your faithfulness to us with our faithfulness to you, and to your ruthless pursuit of us with our ruthless pursuit of you.

Cause us to respond to your love with our love. Remind us today that we love you—that we are committed to you, that we are faithful to you, and that we pursue you—because you first loved us, and because you still love us.

Amen.

- SUNDAY 50 -

The Lord's Day

Renew in us today, O God, the joy of our salvation.

Lead us away from a shallow and faulty understanding of joy, one that thinks of joy as being dependent on a lack of suffering or an absence of struggle or on a surplus of ease or an abundance of pleasure.

Lead us toward a mature and accurate understanding of joy that knows true joy comes from an awareness of your grace, from the fact that you are working your purposes out, and from our participation in the kind of life to which Jesus calls us and for which he shows us the way.

On this Lord's Day, O God, renew in us the joy of our salvation.

Amen.

- SUNDAY 51 -

The Lord's Day

Any sane person would like for there to be peace on earth; we would like to experience a time when there is no conflict anywhere between any nations or, for that matter, between any people.

We recognize that such peace is something for which we should hope and pray and work, inspired by the presence with us of the Prince of Peace, even as we acknowledge that it will not come fully until he comes again finally.

So Lord, to begin where we are, we ask that on this Lord's Day you would remind us of the peace that is ours and that you would enlarge that peace in us—the peace that is wholeness and well-being we experience deep in our being regardless of what rages all around us, the peace that is a gift from you in Jesus Christ our Lord.

Lead us today to know and to celebrate peace in us, even as we commit ourselves anew to work for it and toward it in our community and in our world.

Amen.

- SUNDAY 52 -

The Lord's Day

In every birth a life is potential; in every birth a death is inevitable.

How the life will be lived we're excited to find out; how the death will be died we're better off not knowing.

On this Lord's Day we remember not only the birth of the Savior, but also the life that was potential in his birth and the death that was inevitable in it.

Thank you for it all.

Fill us with a sense of the wonder and mystery of it.

Lead us to know better what his birth, life, and death mean for our birth, life, and death.

Amen.

Monday Prayers

- MONDAY 1 -

Forward

As I look forward,

align my plans with your purpose;
transform my fears with your faithfulness;
expand my view with your vision;
dissolve my guilt with your grace.

And

fill my poverty with your plenty, even as you replace my plenty with your poverty.

Amen.

- MONDAY 2 -

Bread

We don't live by bread alone, Jesus reminds us.

Still, you made us so that we need bread to live; Jesus even taught us to pray so that you would give us the bread we need.

So Father, please give us our daily bread; please give us the bread we need.

Thank you that we can taste and enjoy our bread.

But Lord, guard our appetites. Keep our enjoyment from becoming dependence, our fill from becoming gluttony, our nourishment from becoming obsession.

And as we eat our bread, O Lord, remind us of those who are hungry and malnourished, not so we can feel guilty about what we have to eat but so we will remember to take less for ourselves so we can share more with others.

Amen.

- MONDAY 3 -
Neighbors

O Lord,

The extent of tragedies can be overwhelming—

communities devastated;
people killed, hurt, homeless, and missing;
dwellings and buildings destroyed.

Sometimes we say it feels like our world is falling apart, figuratively speaking; sometimes it does, literally.

Free us from the paralysis of inaction, from the easy assumption there is nothing we can do. Cause us to pray for the victims, for the first responders, for the relief agencies and workers. Move us to give of our abundance or of our little for the sake of those who have nothing.

And Lord, while we pray and give for the sake of hurting strangers in faraway places, keep us aware of the need to pray for and to give of ourselves for the sake of the stranger—not to mention the family member, the co-worker, the neighbor, the friend—who is at our elbow.

Help us to be a neighbor to those way over yonder.
Help us to be a neighbor to this one right here.

Amen.

- MONDAY 4 -
Our Father

"Our Father"—that is how your Son told us to address you in prayer.

Thank you for the word and the reality "Father." Remind us today that

you love us;
you care for us;
you nurture us;
you come to us;

you discipline us;
you hold us;
you let us go;
you welcome us back.

Thank you also for the word and the reality "our." Remind us today that

we do not stand alone;
we do not kneel alone;
we have sisters and brothers;
we need and are needed;
we lean on and are leaned on;
we challenge and are challenged;
we suffer together;
we rejoice together.

Thank you that we—the Holy Trinity, the church local and universal, and the saints in heaven—are today and every day a community of prayer and worship.

Amen.

- MONDAY 5 -
Curves

The week stretches out ahead of me like a road filled with curves; I cannot even see around the first curve, much less all the others.

That is not cause for fear, though, Lord; it is just a needed reminder that my life is in your hands.

So fill me with trust in you, O Lord, with radical trust that will enable me to live boldly.

For this could be a week that makes all the difference for me or for someone else or for my corner of the Kingdom,

but only if I walk the road, my hand in yours—one curve at a time.

Amen.

- MONDAY 6 -
Speaking

Today I will speak words—lots and lots of words.

They don't all have to be meaningful or insightful or important; some of them will be for fun or for mischief or for nothing much at all.

Some of them will be discardable and disposable.

But some of them will be important, and they will need to be insightful and meaningful because someone will depend on them to make a difference to them or to someone they love with whom they want desperately to have a good word to share.

Those words need to have something of your Word in them.

So Lord, thank you for the grace to speak light words and for the grace to speak weighty words.

May the light ones do me good.

May the weighty ones do someone else good.

Amen.

- MONDAY 7 -
Change

O Lord,

We are

recipients of your grace,
vessels of your Spirit,
containers of your love.

We are

the people of God,
the church of the Lord,
the body of Christ.

Because of what we have and because of who we are—because of who you are to us and in us and through us—change us, Lord.

Help us to grow toward who you mean us to be.
Help us to be open to your way for us.
Help us to embrace the difference you make in our lives.

And they'll know we are Christians by our love.

Amen.

- MONDAY 8 -
Legacy

Everyone is unique. Everyone is her or his own person.

We like to say things like that, and to a certain extent and from a certain perspective they are true.

And yet we carry within us—all of us do—a little bit, and sometimes even a big bit, of the people who a long time ago or just a little while ago touched us just once or maybe for a long time and thereby left that bit of themselves with us.

Teachers, mentors, parents, pastors, bosses, authors, artists, colleagues—friends they were, and their influence may have been for better and/or for worse, but insofar as we know they were trying; their hearts were in more or less the right place; they were operating out of love.

We forgive the worse.

We thank you for the better.

We thank you for them.

And we humbly ask, O Lord, that as we leave a bit of ourselves with those who are looking to us and counting on us that they will be able to look back one day and, if they must, forgive the worse and, if they are able, thank you for the better.

May the better far, far, far, far outweigh the worse.

Amen.

- MONDAY 9 -
Waiting

We will spend much time this week waiting—

waiting in line,
waiting at drive-throughs,
waiting at stop lights,
waiting at the doctor's or dentist's office,
waiting for someone—

waiting for something that might change everything.

O Lord, as we wait this week, help us to use that time well—

to converse,
to think,
to reflect,
to pray.

Help us to use our waiting time as learning and training time, so that we might be reminded we are to wait on you to come to us in your time and in your way and that while we wait we can be patient and receptive, always growing in our trust in and reliance on you, the One whose coming changes everything.

Amen.

- MONDAY 10 -
Help

Today, O Lord, like all days, I need your help.

I need your help

to live,
to live well,
to live fully,
to live sacrificially,
to live unselfishly,
to live faithfully.

Today, O Lord, like all days, others need my help.

They need my help

to be acknowledged,
to be encouraged,
to be forgiven,
to be nurtured,
to be embraced,
to be loved.

O Lord, give me a spirit today that is willing to be helped and to help.

Amen.

- MONDAY 11 -
Bodies

Forgive me, Lord, for the mistake I sometimes make of trying to separate my spiritual self from my physical self, as if I can somehow serve you with my spirit while I do less than that with my body.

After all, I am my body and my body is me. I am in the world as my body and the world confronts me in my body, so that is just the way it is and there is no sense in denying it or trying to avoid it.

It's a challenge and so the temptation to escape the challenge by appealing to some supposedly higher nobility in my spirit is very real.

Please lead me away from temptation.

Help me instead to offer my total self—mind and spirit, emotions and motivations, consciousness and unconsciousness, inactions and actions—all of which are realized and exercised right here in this body of mine—in service to you and in service to others.

May my life in my body—which is after all the only life I have—be pleasing to you and helpful to others.

Amen.

- MONDAY 12 -

Worn

We get worn down, Lord, and sometimes it is because

we expend energy on trivial things,
we fret anxiously over useless things,
we spend time on unimportant things,
we use up life on life-draining things,
we focus mostly on our things.

And that's our fault.

We get worn down, Lord, and sometimes it is because

the world is tough,
events seem senseless,
people are problematic,
tragedies are numbing,
our hearts get broken.

And that's not our fault.

We need your help, Lord, so that

hope can stay alive,
enthusiasm can be rekindled,
perseverance can be experienced,
love can be offered,
life can be shared.

And that's our prayer.

So give us, oh Lord, the mind—the motives, the drive, the grace, the love—of Christ so that we might keep moving forward, doing our best to live for you and for others, until we get all the way home.

Amen.

- MONDAY 13 -

Peace

We can't control the actions of others, much less their thoughts or motives or emotions. We have enough trouble with our own.

Nevertheless, we are responsible for which dynamics within us we choose to empower through the cultivation and nurture of them and for the behaviors and actions we choose to practice in light of those developing dynamics.

So Lord, help our relationship, our state of being, with you, with ourselves, and with others to become more and more whole and sound, and help that wholeness and soundness to be exhibited in the ways we act toward you, toward ourselves, and toward others.

May we act

less out of brokenness and more out of wholeness,
less out of sickness and more out of wellness,
less out of need and more out of fulfillment,
less out of fear and more out of trust,
less out of alienation and more out of fellowship.

Amen.

- MONDAY 14 -

Home

With every passing second we grow older.
With every passing moment we draw closer to home.

The realization, obvious as it is, is a little scary when we stop and think about it; on the other hand, it's really quite exciting when we really stop and think about it. After all, home is where the heart is—and our hearts are with you; still, in a very real way your heart is with us—you make your home with us. So in a way we're headed home; in a way we're already home.

Thank you, Lord, that as long as we are with you and you are with us, whether on this side or the side of that final closing of our eyes, we are at home.

Amen.

- MONDAY 15 -

Dark/Light

In the dark, things happen.

Time passes;
the world turns;
sleep occurs.

In the dark, things happen

without our active participation,
so we close our eyes
and we trust it will be all right.

We trust you.

Here in the light of day, things happen.

The difference is that we have something to do with it;
we have something to do in it.

We have to go into it with our eyes wide open.

Help us here in the light

as we do what we can,
as we do what we should,
as we do what we must

to trust you

like we do in the dark.

Amen.

- MONDAY 16 -
Eyes

By your grace, Lord, we opened our eyes this morning.

Help us by your grace to keep them open all day long.

Keep them open to

the wonders of your creation,
the intricacies of nature,
the blessings of our humanity,
the presence of others.

Keep them open to

the realities of life,
the suffering of the oppressed,
the problems of the poor,
the pain of the wounded.

Cause us to see who is there and what is there.
Cause us to live with what we must.
Cause us to address with your grace and love what we can.

Help us to see clearly, Lord, and to live appropriately in light of what we see.

Amen.

- MONDAY 17 -
Trust/Hope Present/Future

To trust is to believe in the present; to hope is to believe in the future. To trust is to believe that you are working your purposes out in the here and now; to hope is to believe that you will work your purposes out in the there and then.

Fill us, O Lord, with trust in you that enables us to live faithfully and boldly right now, knowing the present is in your hands. Fill us, O Lord, with hope in you that enables us to live faithfully and boldly going forward, knowing the future is in your hands.

Amen.

- MONDAY 18 -

Decisions

We make some decisions reflexively and without thinking about them because our identity is in some ways deeply ingrained.

We make other decisions after some brief consideration because the rightness and wrongness of the options seem clear.

We make still other decisions, though, only after much agonizing internal debate because the choice is not between good and bad but rather between good and better or between better and best, and the lines dividing those relative merits can be thin indeed.

Some decisions once made we give no further thought.
Some decisions we never feel good about.

Help us, Lord, on this day and on all days, to seek your guidance in our decision-making by relying on your Spirit in us.

Help us always to be growing into the kind of people who will make decisions out of an identity and a character that are developing in line with your will and way.

Help us in our decision-making to be motivated by grace, love, and a servant spirit.

Help us, once our difficult decisions are made, to do the really hard thing of accepting and living in your peace.

Amen.

- MONDAY 19 -

The Day

This could be the day for someone.

It could be the day for

the cashier at the store,
the child in my classroom,
the client with whom I meet,
the customer in my business,
the co-worker in my office, or
the companion in my travels.

It could be the day when

she finds some hope to grasp, or
he experiences the love he needs, or
she catches a glimpse of the way things are, or
he perceives the calling in his life, or
she finds herself beginning to trust, or
he is nudged by the grace of God.

This could be the day for someone whose life my life will touch.

O God, make me fully present to every person in every place in every moment today because this could be the day for one of them.

Of course, it could also be the day for me.

Amen.

- MONDAY 20 -

Yes

Today, like all days, will be full of questions to which we must respond.

Help us, Lord, to say "Yes" to those questions that merit a positive answer.

"Should I embrace my life in all its aspects?" deserves a "Yes."
"Should I be grateful?" deserves a "Yes."
"Should I be faithful in my relationships?" deserves a "Yes."
"Should I trust you for everything in every situation?" deserves a "Yes."
"Should I love you with all that I am?" deserves a "Yes."
"Should I love others as I love myself?" deserves a "Yes."
"Should I love myself?" deserves a "Yes."
"Should I give up my life so that I can gain it?" deserves a "Yes."
"Should I be more interested in serving than in being served?" deserves a "Yes."
"Should I forgive others as you have forgiven me?" deserves a "Yes."
"Should I follow Jesus Christ as Lord?" deserves a "Yes."

There are many other questions to which we should say "Yes" on this day and on all days.

Help us, Lord, to say "Yes."

Amen.

- MONDAY 21 -

Gratefulness

O God, give us grateful and thankful hearts.

Cause us to live grateful and thankful lives.

At the same time, prevent our gratefulness from turning to pride and our thankfulness to selfishness.

Cause us to show our gratitude and our thankfulness through generosity and sharing and sacrifice.

Then shall our thanks be thanks indeed.

Amen.

- MONDAY 22 -

Forward

When this day is done, we will have moved forward, if in no other sense than that we will have moved one day closer to our conclusion.

Such movement forward is inevitable and runs the risk of being purposeless.

O God, please help us to move forward in areas much more important than the chronological. Help us to move forward

in trust,
in forgiveness,
in peace,
in grace,
in love.

Such movement forward is not inevitable; it requires intentionality. And it is filled with purpose; it requires resolve.

Cause us today to seek—rather, to pursue—movement forward in the areas that matter most.

Amen.

- MONDAY 23 -

Fall

When we fall it can be painful. It can also be embarrassing whether anyone sees it or not.

The real damage from a fall can come in two ways: first, if we think about it too much so that fear comes to rule us and second, if we stay down.

O God, when we fall, help us to get up, and help us not to look back any more than is necessary to learn our lesson.

Amen.

- MONDAY 24 -
Lavishness

Your gifts to us, O God, are—to put it as accurately as we can but at the same time to fall far short of the whole truth—lavish.

Life itself is a lavish gift—to have been given the privilege to be here, to be human, and to be aware.

But you went far beyond that lavishness in giving us in these lives each other as family and friends and companions on the journey.

Being with others and being known by others is lavishness beyond lavishness.

And Lord, you went beyond even that extreme lavishness when you placed within us and among us a sense of you and a desire to know you and to love you, thereby giving us the possibility of relating to you.

For such lavishness upon lavishness upon lavishness, what can we do but praise you and love you—lavishly?

Amen.

- MONDAY 25 -
Resist

There are lots of things we need to resist, but the first thing that comes to mind is temptation. So Lord, help us to resist temptation—and we all have to answer for ourselves as to which temptations are for us the most tempting. And help us to resist the temptation not to be honest about that.

When we fail to resist, forgive us.

And when we don't fail to resist a particular temptation but then fail to resist the temptation to congratulate ourselves on our victory—which, after all, leads to the sin of pride which, in turn, leads to yet another failure—forgive us.

Above all, help us to resist the temptation not to take you into account in absolutely everything.

Amen.

- MONDAY 26 -

X

Traditionally the letter "X" has been used as a symbol for Christ because the Greek word when transliterated into English is *Xristos.*

We also sometimes use the letter "X" as a verb, as in "She X'd out that item from her list."

We also sometimes use the letter "X" to designate a goal, as in "X marks the spot."

We praise you, O God, that in *Xristos* our sins have been X'd out and that, by your grace, our lives are moving toward the goal of being finally and fully found in him.

Amen.

- MONDAY 27 -

Surrender

Our tendency is to fight for what is important to us, and often that is what we should do.

So it runs against our grain, Lord, to find that the most important victories in life can be won only through surrender.

The only way to a whole relationship with you that will lead to a growing awareness of peace, to an increasing sense of purpose, and to a maturing participation in eternal life is the way of surrender to you.

For it is in giving ourselves up that we find ourselves, and it is in giving up our efforts to be righteous that we receive the grace to become righteous.

So we surrender, Lord.

Forgive us for our failure to surrender.

Amen.

- MONDAY 28 -

Linger

There is so much to do; there are so many tasks to be accomplished; there are so many responsibilities to fulfill.

We live in such a rush that sometimes we fail even to notice the beautiful, the gracious, the lovely, and the interesting things that drop unbidden and undeserved into our lives—much less to linger over them.

Help us today, O Lord, not only to notice them but also to linger over them, to take the time to enjoy them and to make room to appreciate them.

Slow us down, Lord; cause us to linger.

Amen.

- MONDAY 29 -

One

We confess our tendency toward divided loyalties, Lord—our inclination to have other gods beside you and sometimes even in front of you.

We affirm that there is to be for us one and only one loyalty, which is our loyalty to you.

Forgive us when we even momentarily allow something or someone to ease or to charge into the place that is rightfully yours alone.

Help us in each and every moment to keep our hearts and minds and lives focused on loving and serving and following you. Help us to submit every aspect of our being to our one supreme loyalty.

Give us a single-minded devotion to you, the one true God.

Amen.

- MONDAY 30 -
Faithful

In our lives we make commitments, and when we make commitments we are saying that the person or persons to whom we are making the commitment can count on us to be faithful.

The best relationship is one in which both parties are faithful.

The absolutely best relationship is one in which both parties are faithful not because they have to be or because they promised to be but because in their heart of hearts, motivated by love, they really want to be.

So help us, Lord, to be faithful to our relationships with you, with our spouses, with our children, with our fellow Christians, with our fellow human beings, and with all to whom we are committed and to whom we are responsible.

May our faithfulness be inspired and informed and empowered by yours.

Amen.

- MONDAY 31 -
Retreat

It is a good thing to get away.

Thank you, O God, for those extended sabbaths; for those times away when we can intentionally set things aside and lay them down so that we can remember they are ultimately in your hands anyway and so that we can be better equipped to take them up again when we go back to them.

Thank you, Lord, for times of retreat. Compel us to take them.

Thank you, Lord, for those responsibilities to which we return. Energize us in our return to them.

And remind us that we never retreat from our main responsibilities: to love you and to love others.

Amen.

- MONDAY 32 -
Surrounded

We are surrounded, so we may as well come out with our hands up.

We are surrounded by the love of the Father.
We are surrounded by the grace of the Son.
We are surrounded by the provision of the Holy Spirit.
We are surrounded by the hosts of heaven.
We are surrounded by the great cloud of witnesses.

Therefore, surrender is appropriate—surrender to all of the help the good Lord makes available to us.

O God, help us today to be constantly aware of how you have surrounded us with all we need to live. Empower us to surrender to your gracious help.

Amen.

- MONDAY 33 -
Plans

We have made plans for this day and for the days ahead.

Bless, O Lord, our plans, insofar as they have been made in humility rather than in arrogance, in faith rather than in presumption, and in hope rather than in fear.

Forgive us, O Lord, if in the making of our plans we have gotten ahead of your timetable or if we have failed to consider how our lives might fit into your larger purposes.

We confess that we cannot know what the next minute, much less the next hour or week or month or year or decade, holds.

We acknowledge that it is irresponsible not to use the best wisdom we can to make the best plans we can.

And we affirm that, whether or not we are as sensitive to them as we ought to be, your purposes and guidance, not to mention circumstances, are going to affect and change our plans.

So make us open and flexible and patient.

So fill us with excitement over the mystery and possibility in it all.

Amen.

- MONDAY 34 -
School

It's the time of year when schools go back into session, so right now those who offer education and those who seek it are preparing for their joint endeavors.

Lord, bless everyone involved in the process of education:

students,
teachers,
administrators,
staff,
paraprofessionals,
parents/family.

May their partnership be productive and beneficial to everyone involved.

Grant that the students' minds will be inquisitive, their hearts will be open, their incentive will be strong, and their families will be nurturing.

Grant that the teachers' hearts will be inspired, their spirits will be patient, their sensitivity will be deep, and their concern will be bountiful.

Grant that the administrators' and staff members' motivation will be strong, their interest will be high, their purpose will be clear, and their relationships will be sound.

Cause the process of education to be so effective, Lord, that at the end of the year everyone involved will know they have grown in intellect and in character.

Amen.

- MONDAY 35 -
Alert

We all know what it is like to be walking alone after dark. Our senses are heightened so that we are alert to every sound and to every movement anywhere around us; in our fear we will even hear and see things that are not there.

Lord, make us alert as we walk through this day; heighten our senses so that we are fully alert to everything going on around us.

Make us alert to

the lives of other people,
the crises of our community,
the resources for help that are available,
the ways in which you are working,
the signs of your presence in the world.

At the same time, Lord, protect us from the fear and anxiety that would cause us to waste our time and energy worrying about what is not there and thus not real.

Heighten our senses, O Lord; keep us alert to the things that matter because they are the things about which you would have us do something in partnership with you and with others.

Amen.

- MONDAY 36 -
Temptation

O God,

Lead us not into temptation; deliver us from evil.
Lead us instead into wholeness; deliver us into goodness.

We can often—perhaps even usually—find the strength within ourselves to resist the temptation to do a bad thing; perhaps we don't, but we can.

But that's a small victory because what we can't do is to form and shape our own hearts into the kind of hearts that are so full of love and grace and forgiveness and devotion—that are so full of you—that they find such temptations untempting.

So God, fill our hearts with you; fill our lives up with the desire to be one way—to be fully in love with you—and to do one thing—to show that love in every possible way.

It is not enough for us not to do bad things.

We want to be people whose hearts are becoming so full of good—of your kind of good—that there is less and less room for the bad.

Lead us not into temptation; deliver us from evil.
Lead us instead into wholeness; deliver us into goodness.

Amen.

- MONDAY 37 -
Wisdom

Give us wisdom today and all days, Lord.

Give us the ability to navigate the journey of these lives with your grace and love and teachings as our compass.

Give us the courage to try to discern your ways for us and to live in those ways, but at the same time give us humility to know we do not always discern those ways just right.

Give us the grace to respect all others who are in good faith trying to find your way for them, too, even when their trying leads them down paths we do not choose.

Give us the insight, Lord, to know that while in some ways your wisdom is far beyond our ability to comprehend, you in your grace caused that wisdom to be embodied in Jesus Christ of whom we can read and to whom we can look and who, through your Holy Spirit, we can experience in our lives.

So may we be wise enough to learn from and to follow him.

Amen.

- MONDAY 38 -

Period

As a mark of punctuation, a period is misleading because it purports to mark the end of something when in fact it does not because it cannot.

Oh, a period can mark the end of a sentence, so in that sense it is legitimate, but it cannot bring an end to the narrative of which a sentence is a part. Even when a sentence is the last one in a novel, for example, the final period in the book cannot stop the continuation of the story that goes on in the reader's mind.

There is no end to words.
There is no end to narrative.
There is no end to story.

Lord, forgive us for our desire to place periods in our lives, to try to achieve finality or to arrive at completion while we are still in the middle of the telling—in the living—of our story.

Inspire us to live fully all the way through to the end of our earthly sojourn.

And remind us of the great truth that even when we reach the end of our narrative on earth and the period is seemingly put on the last sentence of our story, that story does in fact go on through the people and the memories we leave behind and through our eternal living in your presence.

Amen.

- MONDAY 39 -

Semicolon

A semicolon separates parts of a sentence that are separate but nonetheless related.

Help us, Lord, to tend well to the semicolons in our lives, which primarily have to do with our relationships with other people.

On the one hand we are related to absolutely everyone we know or don't know, we see or don't see; we are made of the same stuff as they are, we ultimately have the same ancestors they have, we were created by the same God they were, and the same Savior died for them as died for us.

On the other hand, we are separate from even those with whom we have the closest relationships, including our spouses, our children, and our parents; every other person in the world, whether they sleep with us or came out of us or live in a place we've never seen and speak a language we've never heard, is to us the other.

So Lord, help us to accept and to celebrate and to work with the otherness of all others. Everyone else is separate from us, and we need to treat them as valued individuals and as mysteries beyond our comprehension whose uniqueness is a gift to them and to us all.

Help us also to accept and to celebrate and to work with our relationship to all others. Everyone else is our sister or brother, and we need to be there for each other and to accept our responsibility to each other. Some we will never know, and even those we know best we can know only partially. But what a blessing it is to know and to be known, to accept and to be accepted, to embrace and to be embraced, to love and to be loved.

Amen.

- MONDAY 40 -

Parents

In some cases our parents have been long with us. We're in our seventies, and one or both of them are now in their nineties, for example.

In other cases our parents have been long gone. We're in our fifties, and one or both of them have been dead for years or even for decades, for example.

In some cases we barely remember our parents; in other cases our memories are mainly of their abuse or neglect of us; and in yet other cases our memories are so positively selective that our parents were better parents than any parents possibly could be.

In any case, Lord, help us to honor our parents; help us to give them appropriate weight and value and importance.

Help us to honor them in the ways we treat them. If they are still with us, help us to respect them, to listen to them, to be with them, to take them seriously, and to care for them in ways that will show our love and promote their dignity.

Help us to honor them in the ways we live out our parental roles. Whether they are still with us or not, help us to take the best of the ways they parented us and to leave the worst. Help us to honor and to redeem their parenting by being better parents than they were—whether that means being almost completely different or only slightly improved.

May our parenting be such that it will be an honor for our children to honor us.

Amen.

- MONDAY 41 -
Limitations

Thank you, O God, for our limitations, for it would be an unbearable burden if we could do anything and handle everything; because if we could, then people would expect us to do so.

Forgive us for our sometimes unwillingness to accept our limitations, an unwillingness birthed by our arrogance. If we go too far down that road, we are trying to be our own god—which is the essence of sin.

Besides, it is in the recognition, acknowledgement, and acceptance of our limitations that we find much freedom and much grace. It is at the limits of our abilities and capabilities that we find others whose abilities and capabilities complement and extend ours. It is at the place where there seems to be absolutely nothing we or anyone else can do that we find you.

Our limitations are among our greatest blessings.

Give us the wisdom to know and to live that truth.

Amen.

- MONDAY 42 -
Blessed

It is usually easy to consider ourselves blessed when most or all is well; it is usually hard to consider ourselves blessed when some or most is difficult.

Give us the wisdom, Lord, to know that sometimes when most or all is well, we are actually in a potentially precarious position because of our tendency to fall lazily into the habits of inactive ease that do not promote our spiritual health; and that sometimes when some or most is difficult, we are actually in a potentially positive position because of the opportunity to rely energetically on the habits of active response that do promote our spiritual health.

We do not ask for an irrational mind that tells us bad is good and good is bad.

We do ask for a maturing faith that creates in us an expanded understanding of what it means to be "blessed," meaning we are blessed when we in all times and in all circumstances intentionally and consistently live in light of the fact that you are with us in all of it.

Amen.

- MONDAY 43 -
Ideas

Today we will have ideas; we will come up with images or plans or concepts to address some problem or situation or need.

Some ideas form after much deliberation and consideration, while others seem to pop up unbidden out of nowhere. They emerge from some combination of what is within us and what we encounter outside ourselves and ultimately, we hope and trust, from you—at least the good ones do.

And some of our ideas are good ones, but some of our ideas are bad ones.

Thank you, Lord, for the ability to form ideas.

Grant that we will have more good ones than bad ones.

Give us the wisdom to discern the good ideas from the bad, the courage to act on the good ones, and the willingness to forget the bad ones.

And may we ask of all of our ideas whether they pass the test of love for you and love for our neighbors.

Amen.

- MONDAY 44 -
Impasse

Today we are likely to face an impasse, a seeming dead end, a roadblock around or through which there is no obvious passage.

Give us wisdom, Lord, to be able to tell a real impasse from a seeming one; we are prone to treat minor hindrances as major obstacles.

When we are faced with a legitimate impasse, give us appropriate insight into how we should deal with it.

If it is something that should be accepted and lived with, give us peace about accepting and living with it.

If it is something through or around which a way must be found, give us the courage and creativity to find that way and the tenacity to keep trying until we find it.

If it is something with which we cannot deal alone, give us grace to seek and to accept the help of others.

We thank you, Lord, for the challenges with which life presents us. May every impasse increase our trust in you and our awareness of your gracious provision.

Amen.

- MONDAY 45 -
Conversations

Chances are that we will become engaged in conversations today; O Lord, keep us open in those moments so that we can give to our partners in conversation and receive from them as well.

As we give and receive information, let it be true information we are sharing.

As we give and receive opinions, let it be honest opinions we are sharing.

As we give and receive advice, let it be heartfelt advice we are sharing.

And always, Lord, as we give of ourselves and to each other, let it be our genuine selves—insofar as we can know them—we are sharing.

Amen.

- MONDAY 46 -
Us

Everyone belongs to more than one "us."

Male or female—that's us.
Black or white or brown—that's us.
Asian or European or African—that's us.
Christian or Muslim or Jewish—that's us.
Liberal or conservative or moderate—that's us.
Rich or poor or middle-class—that's us.
Rural or urban or suburban—that's us.

It's funny how much of what determines and defines our "us" is accidental—in the sense it happened to us with no effort or choice on our part; race and place and family of origin just happen to us, for example.

Help us, Lord, to take neither inordinate pride nor to find inordinate shame in those aspects of our group identity in which we had no choice. Help us neither to value nor to devalue ourselves inappropriately because of the groups into which we happened to be born.

Our choices and decisions do have something to do with some of the groups in which we find our identity; we determine and develop philosophies and approaches and mindsets, and then we tend to associate with those who think similarly with the result that we become more and more convinced of the rightness of our positions.

Help us, Lord, to choose wisely when it comes to how we develop our thoughts and attitudes. Help us to maintain a critical approach toward our own ideas and toward those of the groups with which we associate.

And cause us never to forget that our primary "us" is those who are the followers of Jesus Christ our Lord—regardless of the other groups to which we belong.

Amen.

- MONDAY 47 -
Purpose

Some people think everything is happenstance and randomness and accident.

Other people think everything is pre-programmed and pre-determined and pre-set.

Perhaps a little humility and naiveté are in order.

God, I confess that I don't know why things happen like they happen when they happen; I furthermore confess that if I must have such knowledge to know some peace, then peace is the last thing I will know.

And God, I just want to be able to trust in you, to have enough faith to believe that somehow, some way, you are working your purposes out in and through your vast creation as well as in and through my little life.

When it comes to your purposes and to the ways you are fulfilling them, O God, I affirm that I do not understand and that I do believe.

Increase my trust and my understanding—but increase my trust more.

Amen.

- MONDAY 48 -
Awkward

Life is filled with awkward moments, so chances are good that we'll have one today.

Awkward moments occur when something is said that shouldn't have been said or said at the wrong moment or said differently than it was meant or said when we find ourselves in the presence of someone with whom we'd rather not be just now because of some wrong inflicted or perceived or because of some obligation unmet or unacknowledged or because of some expectation unfulfilled or unexpressed or when we get caught in or catch ourselves in some wrong or in some mistake or, perhaps most painfully, in some hypocrisy.

Awkward moments, then, while embarrassing, can also be clarifying; they can help us to see ourselves and our situation more clearly and to acknowledge our humanity more readily.

O God, cause our awkward moments to function as windows through which we get a better look at the way things are or as mirrors in which we get a better look at the way we are.

As appropriate, let them make us cry or let them make us laugh—and help us to know which response is appropriate, because it's really awkward when we get it wrong.

Amen.

- MONDAY 49 -
Fail

Today, O God, when I try and fail, remind me that at least I tried.

Give me strength
so that I might never stop trying.

Give me love
so that I might keep trying in the right direction.

Give me grace
so that I might grow through my failures.

Give me wisdom
so that I might avoid a repetition of my mistakes.

Give me integrity
so that I might accept responsibility for my failures.

Tomorrow, O God, when I try and fail, remind me that at least I tried.

Amen.

- MONDAY 50 -
Aside

O Lord,

In the midst of the hecticness that will mark this day, remind us to turn aside and spend time with you.

In the midst of the work that needs to be done and the tasks that need to be accomplished, remind us to turn aside and spend time with you.

In the midst of the encounters and conversations and controversies we will have with people today, remind us to turn aside and spend time with you.

In the midst of the worries, cares, fears, and anxieties to which if we are not careful we will give ourselves over, remind us to turn aside and to spend time with you.

Given the love we profess to have for you and given the love we claim to know you have for us, it is unfortunate that we have to ask you to remind us to spend time with you—forgive us.

But please, don't stop reminding us.

Amen.

- MONDAY 51 -
Corners

The corner is the place of retreat; it is where the person who is weary of all the activity goes to stand.

The corner is the place of repentance; it is where the child who has done wrong and who needs to think about it and move past it might be sent.

The corner is the place of convergence; it is where the various components of a room come together.

Thank you, God, for corners—we need them.

We need those times and places in our lives in which and to which we retreat to get away from it all, to repent so that we can move in a better direction, and to ponder the ways in which the components of our lives by your grace fit together.

Lead us, Lord, to find and to take advantage of our corners.

But don't let us stay in them.

After all, the corner is also the place from which the fighter comes out fighting.

Amen.

- MONDAY 52 -
Weather

The rain that waters the ground also floods the land.

The snow that blankets the countryside also snarls the city.

The wind that rustles the leaves also batters the buildings.

The love that settles over us also overwhelms us.

O God, what calms has the potential to foment; what moves in has the potential to break out.

Your best gifts, O God, come with an element of significant risk. Help us to be open and brave and daring and, as a result, so full of life that neither we nor those around us can hardly stand it.

Amen.

Tuesday Prayers

- TUESDAY 1 -
Thanks

Thank you, O Lord.

But thanks seem hardly enough when I owe it all to you.

It is easy to say "Thank you" and then to go on my way, thinking more of me than I do of you—or of others.

Overwhelm me—flood me—drown me—in gratitude, so that I may lose myself in it, in you, and in others.

Sweep me this day from words of thanks into a lifestyle of gratitude.

Amen.

- TUESDAY 2 -
For Granted

We take so much for granted, Lord,

the things that come our way
without our bidding
despite our unworthiness
from you—only from you.

We usually don't even think about them and when we do, we all too often think with fear of losing them rather than with amazement over having them, rather than with faith that we'll have them for as long as we need them.

Don't let us take it for granted, too, Lord,

the faith that comes our way
without our bidding
despite our unworthiness

from you—only from you.

Amen.

- TUESDAY 3 -

Dullness

Deliver us from dullness, O Lord, the dullness that sets in when we fail

to appreciate your astounding creation;
to be vulnerable and genuine in our relationships with family and friends;
to be open to other people, other ideas, other cultures, and other possibilities;

to read and study Scripture with the goal of being formed in the image of Christ;
to pray with our hearts set only on being in your loving presence;
to submit ourselves to each other out of reverence for Christ;

to take the occasional risk because faithfulness and faith seem to demand it;
to remember and to live in light of the facts that Christ is in us, we are the body of Christ in the world, and the kingdom of heaven is among us.

Deliver us from dullness, O Lord, and give us over instead to the excitement that comes from knowing you are you and we are yours.

Amen.

- TUESDAY 4 -

Need

O Lord,

We are your beloved children, your chosen people, your prized possession, the apple of your eye.

You made us a little lower than the angels. You made us in your image. You love us so much that your only begotten Son died for us while we were yet sinners.

We will need to remember all of that today because today it will again be obvious to us, if not to those around us, that

we are broken,
we are wounded,
we are weak,

even as we try so hard to act like it is not so.

Remind us that we have this treasure in earthen vessels, your strength is made known in our weakness and that, while by his stripes we are healed, his scars still show and so will ours.

But by your grace you will work with them and through them so that others will see you in us.

Help us today not to deny how in need of your grace we are, for it is the poor in spirit, your Son told us, to whom belongs the kingdom of heaven.

Amen.

- TUESDAY 5 -
Lessons

In the events of this day, O Lord, there will be lessons to be learned.
Help me to learn them.

When I lie down tonight, may I be able to look back on this day with
the knowledge that

I am more me,
I am more authentically me,
I am more what you intend for me to be

than I was when the day began.

I can't know in advance what the lessons are that I need to learn today,
but experience teaches me that I always need to learn

to trust more,
to help more,
to forgive more,
to listen more,
to expect more,
to pray more and—especially—
to love more.

May I learn my lessons well today, O Lord. And may it show in the way
I live tomorrow, even as I go out to learn more lessons.

Amen.

- TUESDAY 6 -
Teachers

Thank you, Lord, for the teachers who taught us.
Where would we be without them?

Thank you, Lord, for the teachers who teach our children.
Thank you for their dedication and their commitment.
Thank you for their sacrifice and for their courage.
Thank you, Lord, for their love.

They do superhuman work, Lord, but they are nonetheless only human.
They have the struggles and joys and sorrows and defeats and victories and trials and triumphs and gains and losses—they have all the experiences, good and bad—the rest of us have.

And they carry all of that with them as they teach our children.

Please, Lord, bless them.
Please, Lord, strengthen them.
Please, Lord, encourage them.
Please, Lord, enliven them.

Please, Lord, let them feel your love and grace on this day and on all days.

Amen.

- TUESDAY 7 -
Passion

O God, give us passion—

such a love for our place and purpose in the world,
such a drive to live in service to you and to others,
such a sense of calling that we must press on no matter what the cost—

that every day we will give it all we have.

We speak of our Lord's Passion as the events that led to his death on the cross.

It may be that following our passion will cost us a lot—maybe everything—too.

If so—so be it.

It will be worth it to know, at the end of our lives, that we really lived.

Amen.

- TUESDAY 8 -
Gratitude

Lord, I am grateful, but I think my gratitude needs to be expanded.

For example:

I am grateful when I succeed, but I need to be grateful for the chance to try.

I am grateful when people like me and when I like them, but I need to be grateful for people in all their complexity.

I am grateful when things go smoothly, but I need to be grateful for the rough times that help me grow.

I am grateful when I feel you near, but I need to be grateful that you are near.

So today, O Lord, I would be grateful for an expansion of my gratitude, but I am grateful for the realization that I need it.

Amen.

- TUESDAY 9 -

Basics

Thank you, O God, for the basics of life—

the ground on which we stand,
the air we breathe,
the water we drink,
the food we eat,
the shelter we have,
the people we love,
the grace we know.

Make and keep us mindful of those for whom

the ground is threatening,
the air is dirty,
the water is infested,
the food is limited,
the shelter is inadequate,
the people are manipulative,
the grace is unfelt.

May our thanks for the basics spill over into efforts to share out of our abundance with those for whom they are in short supply.

Then shall our thanks be thanks indeed.

Amen.

- TUESDAY 10 -

Weary

Sometimes it all catches up with us, with the result that something beyond tiredness—something that is the accumulation of all our tiredness—sets in and we are beset by weariness.

It comes from our tendency to expend too much energy on peripheral things, and to spend too much of our lives on things that are not best, and to fret too much over things that are better left in your hands.

Lord,
revive and renew us today and every day;
fill us with a hope that will be the spark of life within us;
cause us to turn away from habits and attitudes that promote weariness;
cause us to turn toward the kind of life that will nourish rather than drain our spirits—

a life that puts you first, others second, and self last;
a life that focuses on trying to do your will;
a life that takes time to commune with you;
a life that knows how to let go;
a life that lives out its God-given passion.

Amen.

- TUESDAY 11 -
Transformation

It is so easy—too easy—to go along with our culture, to blend in with our surroundings, to think and talk and act in the ways everyone expects.

It is so easy—too easy—to be a spiritual, social, and ethical chameleon and, like a chameleon, to blend in for our own protection.

Help us, Lord, to take full advantage of the opportunity we have in you to be changed, to be transformed, to be made different; to have our hearts, our minds, our motives, our wills, and our actions changed by you and, best of all, to have them become more like those of Christ.

But if we are changed, if we are transformed, if we are made different, we will stand out and in standing out we will become more vulnerable.

Remind us of and strengthen us with the truth that, ultimately speaking, there is no safer place to be than in your will, regardless of the danger in which it places us.

Amen.

- TUESDAY 12 -
Endurance

Sometimes it's not easy.
Sometimes life is hard.
Sometimes faith is tested.
Sometimes people are cruel.

In those times we need especially to stay in close touch with you from whom our help comes.

In all times we need to stay in close touch with you so that we will be well positioned to be aware of your presence and help when the hard times come.

So keep us mindful, Lord, that you are working your purposes out, so that we might have a hope that produces joy in all circumstances.

Help us, Lord, when we must suffer, to do so as people of faith, so that we might wait for your deliverance in your time.

Encourage us, Lord, to develop a disciplined life of prayer, so that we might know in every moment you are with us and we with you and that in that relationship we can endure to the end.

Amen.

- TUESDAY 13 -
Mercy

When we get down to it, both justice and mercy are ultimately in your hands, Lord.

It is best that way, of course, because only you know all the facts and only you can see people's hearts.

As for us, when we are wronged or hurt, whether we try to exact revenge or to apply grace and mercy, we will do so in flawed ways.

Frankly, Lord, it seems revenge is easier.

But we acknowledge that you call us to do the harder thing of extending mercy and grace and forgiveness and kindness to those who hurt us.

And if you call us to do it, you will empower us to do it.

We need to be filled up with your grace and mercy and love and forgiveness if we're going to pull that off.

Fill us, Lord.
Help us, Lord.

Amen.

- TUESDAY 14 -
Responsible

There are things to be done today that must be done by me. They are my responsibility and if I don't do them, they won't get done.

There is pressure in that reality
—because I have to.

There is pleasure in that reality
—because I get to.

So Lord, I don't ask you to make me responsible
—because I already am.

I ask you rather to help me to embrace my responsibility as the demand and blessing it is.

I also ask you to protect me from the anxiety that comes from believing it's all up to me and never to let me forget that when all is said and done, it's really all up to you—the knowledge of which frees me up to do my part in freedom and trust.

Amen.

- TUESDAY 15 -
Try

It is wrong for us to live as if the results and the outcomes are in our hands.

Forgive us, Lord, for such pride.
Guard us, Lord, from such anxiety.

It is wrong, too, for us to live as if our efforts and contributions do not matter.

Forgive us, Lord, for such inattention.
Guard us, Lord, from such sloth.

Thank you for the opportunities to make a difference in what lies before us this day. Cause us to take seriously our living so that we might take full advantage of it for our sake, for the world's sake, and for your sake.

We leave the outcomes and results to you.
As for our part, we only ask that we will be inspired to try.

Amen.

- TUESDAY 16 -
Child

I have a clear memory of what it was like, when in my childhood I was afraid, to tell my mother or father of my fear and to have them take me in their arms and hold me and to have descend upon me the sense that not only was it going to be all right but that it *was* all right.

Somehow, their love enveloped me in such a way that my fear was absorbed in it.

Dear Lord, now I am an adult and I am expected by convention and by my peers to stand on my own two feet and to deal with my own fears and worries and stresses.

I confess that I cannot. I confess that I am still a child in need of a parent to hold me and to help me and to absorb my fears in love.

Thank you, Lord, for being that parent. Forgive me when I forget. Cause me to come to you with all that is mine and with all that is me so that you can hold me and help me and love me.

I need you, dear Lord.

I need you.

Amen.

- TUESDAY 17 -
Simple/Complex

In a way, it is so simple: if we want to live a good life, a happy life, a blessed life, then we should walk in your ways—and not in the ways of the wicked—and we should follow the teachings of your Word—and not the advice of sinners.

As simple as that sounds, though, we need help, Lord.

We need help to overcome our tendency too easily and carelessly to conclude that we know what is good and what is bad; what is your way and what is not your way; and what is the meaning, intent, and spirit of your Word and what is not the meaning, intent, and spirit of your Word.

We need help to overcome our tendency to substitute our preferences for your truth, our biases for your direction, and our comforts for your call.

We need help to overcome our tendency to be formed by our legalism rather than your grace, by our rules rather than your liberty, and by our desires rather than your demands.

So give us grace, Lord, to live the simple life of walking in your way and of following your Word.

And give us grace, Lord, to remember it's not as simple as it sounds.

Amen.

- TUESDAY 18 -
Water

The water we have now, I understand, is the same water that was here from the time water got here; it just keeps being recycled. Thank you, God, for such an efficient and ingenious system.

Sometimes, when the floods come, we see the destruction that even a good and essential thing can bring.

Lord, have mercy.

Sometimes, when we pollute our streams and rivers and lakes and oceans,
we see the destruction we will inflict even on a good and essential thing.

Lord, have mercy.

We do a lot of things with water, but at least two of those things give us life.

First, we drink it and are thereby replenished.
Second, we are baptized in it and are thereby renewed.

In one case we take it into ourselves; in the other we are taken into it.

In one case we are made alive physically; in the other we are made alive spiritually.

Help us, Lord, to remember to take plenty of water into our bodies
so that we might be and stay physically whole and strong.

Help us, Lord, to remember we were taken into the water in baptism
so that we might be and stay spiritually whole and strong.

The water reminds us of who we are. Thank you.

Amen.

- TUESDAY 19 -
Motivation

It is a good thing to do our duty, to do the right thing whether we want to do it or not. So help us, Lord, to do what we should when we should.

It is a better thing to do the right thing for the right reason, to do it because our hearts are so full of love for you and for others that we just about can't help ourselves. So help us, Lord, to be who we should be so that we will do what we should do because of love.

Help us to do our duty. But even more, cause us to be filled with your love so that our duty will become joy.

Amen.

- TUESDAY 20 -
No

Today, like all days, will be full of questions to which we must respond. Help us, Lord, to say "No" to those questions that merit a negative answer.

"Should I despair of the way the world is?" deserves a "No."
"Should I keep people at arm's length for the sake of my peace of mind?" deserves a "No."
"Should I look out for myself and let the rest of the world look out for itself?" deserves a "No."
"Should I talk about the problems without working on the solutions?" deserves a "No."
"Should I try to escape the world rather than live fully in it?" deserves a "No."
"Should I fail to be faithful in the disciplines that will put me in a position to receive your comforts and challenges?" deserves a "No."
"Should I be careless in my commitments to God and to people?" deserves a "No."
"Should I forget to thank you for your grace and for all your blessings?" deserves a "No."
"Should I treat anything in my life as if it is not an aspect of my following of Jesus?" deserves a "No."

There are many other questions to which we should say "No" on this day and on all days. Help us, Lord, to say "No."

Amen.

- TUESDAY 21 -

Dead People

It is hard sometimes to come to terms in our lives with people who are dead but who are still alive to us.

It can be hard because we feel something was left undone or some hurt was left unforgiven or some words were left unsaid or some feelings were left unexpressed or some wound was left unhealed.

O God, help us to deal well with our grief.

Help us to accept that all of our relationships—even the best ones—are laced with imperfection.

Help us to live in the peace that comes from remembering people as they really were and from living life as it really is.

Perhaps the only thing harder than coming to terms with people who are dead but who are still alive to us is coming to terms with people who are still alive but who are dead to us.

They may be dead to us because of a broken relationship or they may be dead to us because they belong to a group or a "category" we choose not to accept.

O God, help us to deal well with those people who though alive are dead to us; help us to work to heal broken relationships and to work to understand those whose lives are different in some significant way than ours.

Thank you for your peace; help us to know it in our relationships with those who are gone and with those who are still here.

Amen.

- TUESDAY 22 -

Anger

Help us, Lord, to be honest with ourselves about what makes us angry. Do we get angry mainly over injustices that occur against us or that occur against others?

Help us, Lord, to be filled with and guided by you so that we are angered by the wrongs that anger you. Help us to follow Jesus so closely that we are angered by the kind of wrongs that angered him.

And then help us, Lord, to handle and to act on our anger not in ways that contemplate and seek vengeance but rather in ways that seek to right wrongs and to change lives and to improve situations.

Give us holy and helpful anger, Lord.

Amen.

- TUESDAY 23 -

Grace

It is by grace we are saved.
It is by grace we are sustained.
It is by grace we are being led home.

Grace means we are loved by God because of who God is and not because of who we are and what we do or don't do.

Grace is not only a gift; it is *the* gift.

Cause us, Lord, to celebrate grace, to live in grace, and to be changed by grace.

And cause us to be instruments of your grace in the ways we deal with the people around us—because everyone needs grace.

Amen.

- TUESDAY 24 -

Mystery

As time goes by and progress is made, more and more questions about how things are and how things came to be are answered—and that's a good thing.

We thank you, God, for the work of scientists and other researchers and for the answers they discover to many of our questions. Bless their ongoing work; may we make good and productive use of their discoveries.

But for all the answers that have been found, there is still a profound sense of mystery here in our little corner of the universe—and that's a good thing.

Help us never to lose our sense of awe and wonder at the mystery that something in us—intuition, maybe, or spirit—just seems to know is there.

Thank you for the ways in which you have revealed yourself to us so that you are not utterly mystery to us.

But oh, that awe...that wonder...that sense of the divine—to lose it is to think we grasp you completely and maybe that in grasping you we control you.

That is utter arrogance that leads to utter foolishness. Cause us rather to accept and to live in wonder over the mystery that is you.

Amen.

- TUESDAY 25 -

Solitude

It is good to be alone, to be away from it all, to be away from them all.

Lord, grant us times of solitude; help us to be disciplined in taking regular times to be away and to be alone. Help us also to remember that when we are alone we are not, because you are always with us; help us to cultivate our sense of your presence.

Then help us, Lord, to go from our solitude back to it all, back to them all, refreshed and renewed and empowered to bring your grace and love and power to bear on the needs and the hurts we find as we live in the world.

Amen.

- TUESDAY 26 -

Yonder

Yonder is where we are headed; about all we know about it is that we aren't there yet and that with every second that passes we are a second closer to it.

Your Book tells us about the heavenly yonder that is our ultimate destiny and our final home. Fill us with a yearning for that yonder that will at the same time somehow enliven us for the living of these days.

And fill us with wonder and excitement and faith as we move toward whatever yonder you have for us today and in all the days to come.

Thank you for where we are and for the road we have traveled to get here. Strengthen and inspire us for the journey that will take us to who knows—you know—where.

Amen.

- TUESDAY 27 -

Release

There will come a time for each of us when we will have to let it all go; we will close our eyes for the last time on this earth, and there will be nothing we can do but give ourselves over into your care.

It will be a sweet release.

Help us, Lord, to practice such release today and every day. Help us today and every day to learn a little more about placing our lives in your hands and trusting in your love and care.

If we must release ourselves to you for eternity, it just makes sense for us to release ourselves to you in this world of space and time.

But down here we must make a choice; and how we choose goes a long way toward determining whether or not we know peace, joy, and fulfillment.

So help us, Lord, to choose wisely; help us to choose sweet release here and now.

Amen.

- TUESDAY 28 -
Compassion

How different things would be had you, God, upon seeing the pitiable state of us human beings, felt great compassion arising from your great love and done nothing about it.

Instead, you gave—gave your beloved Son.

Today, like all days, we will see, in images from far away brought to us via print or broadcast or online media and in faces that appear right in front of us right where we live, people whose predicaments will cause us to feel compassion.

Thank you for the love that leads to compassion.

Forgive us when we choose to do nothing about it.

Deliver us from the paralysis that results from the realization we can't do anything about everything.

Help us, inspire us, compel us to do something to help someone.

Amen.

- TUESDAY 29 -
Two

Much of life is an interplay between two: between one person and another person, between a "you" and a "me."

Out of that interplay comes most of what is meaningful—be it filling or draining, enlightening or maddening, encouraging or disheartening—in life.

On the one hand, oh God, we need your help lest we become so desperate to relate to another person that we act out of motives that are less than love and thus not worthy of our humanity or that we accept treatment from another that degrades or belittles us.

On the other hand, oh God, we need your help lest we be so afraid of getting hurt that we fail to be vulnerable enough and open enough and honest enough and bold enough with another to enter into a real relationship with her or him.

Help us, Lord, to grow more and more healthy, sound, and whole in our personhood, in our sense of self, so that we can relate to each other in ways that are more and more healthy, sound, and whole.

In other words, Lord, help us to love one another.

Amen.

- TUESDAY 30 -
Provision

A long time ago, O Lord, you sent bread from heaven to provide what your people needed for their physical hunger.

Later on, you sent the Bread from heaven to provide what all people needed for their spiritual hunger.

We thank you, God, that you give us each day our daily bread and our daily Bread; we thank you that you provide daily and perpetually for our physical and our spiritual needs.

There are people all around us who are still hungry, either in the physical or the spiritual sense or both in the physical and the spiritual senses.

As we thank you for providing for us, show us that and how you intend for us to be the conduits for your provision to others—and then cause us to do so.

Amen.

- TUESDAY 31 -

Tips

It's funny how when a waitress or waiter or other server seems genuinely interested in serving you, you want to leave that person a generous tip. But when a waiter or waitress or other server doesn't seem to care, you have to make yourself leave the person even the industry-promoted and culturally accepted minimum.

You don't even think about the possibility that the eager server is being eager precisely because he or she hopes to get a generous tip or about the possibility that the dour server has something going on in her or his life that may make eager service difficult and that a good tip could help the situation.

It's likely sub-Christian for us to serve God with the hope we'll get a divine big tip for it. It's also likely sub-Christian for us to try to appear eager about our service when we're not or to try to put up any kind of front at all.

O God, we are saved to serve you and we are called to serve you. We recognize that one of the main ways we serve you is through serving others.

Give us hearts that really and truly want to serve.

When our hearts are not eager, give us the discipline to serve as best we can, and cause even that discipline to be motivated by our love for you and for others.

And help us to see the privilege of serving you as reward enough for serving you.

Amen.

- TUESDAY 32 -

Hurts

It's hard to say which cause us the most pain: the hurts others inflict on us or the ones we inflict on others.

It's hard to say which is the more painful question to pose:
"Why did they do that to me?" or "Why did I do that to them?"

Lord, our hurts are some of our heaviest burdens. Give us grace to bear them, to deal with them, and, insofar as it is possible, to move beyond them.

Give us grace to forgive those who have hurt us.

Give others grace to forgive us for hurting them.

Finally—and this may be the hardest grace of all—give us grace to forgive ourselves for the hurts we have inflicted on others and, in the process, on ourselves.

Amen.

- TUESDAY 33 -

Pain

There are all kinds of pains—physical, spiritual, emotional, mental, and societal, for example—and in the course of a life we will know them all.

We do not seek pain, but when it comes we have to do something with it. And if everything in our lives is touched and transformed by the presence of Christ, then that includes our pains.

Help us, Lord, not to deny our pain.
Help us, Lord, not to cover up our pain.
Help us, Lord, not to love our pain.
Help us, Lord, not to nurture our pain.
Help us, Lord, not to cling to our pain.

But help us, Lord, to recognize our pain.

Help us, Lord, to live into our pain.
Help us, Lord, to live through our pain.
Help us, Lord, to learn from our pain.
Help us, Lord, to be transformed through our pain.
Help us, Lord, to find you in our pain.

And help us, Lord, not to let our pain isolate us from others, but let it rather join us to others who are in pain, too.

In the name of the One in whom you entered into our pain,

Amen.

- TUESDAY 34 -
Imperfection

Perfection is not attainable in this life, which is both a frustration and a relief.

It's a frustration because there are ways and areas in which we'd like to get it just right. It's a relief because we need the freedom to make mistakes and because we need room to grow.

Lord, give us the desire to do better, to get better, and to be better in the areas of life that matter most, for example:

our relationship with you and our relationship with others,
our acceptance of grace and our offering of grace,
our reception of forgiveness and our granting of forgiveness,
our gratitude for blessings and our sharing of blessings.

At the same time, Lord, give us the grace to accept that where we are in such areas will never be exactly where we need or want to be.

Thank you for where we are.
Thank you for where we are going.
Thank you for where we will be.

Amen.

- TUESDAY 35 -
Complete

We never catch up; we never finish; we are never completely done.

In a way, that's motivation for us, because it means we always have room to grow and reason to progress; it means we always have reasons to get up in the morning and to do our work each day and to nurture our spirits all the time.

In a way, though, it's a frustration to us, because it means there's no end in sight, because we often don't make the kind of progress we'd like—whether on our projects or on ourselves—and because sometimes weariness sets in.

Lord, give us the wisdom to see that sometimes we do complete some projects and we do often make good progress; help us to acknowledge and to celebrate those small victories.

Give us the faith to know you are working your purposes out and that the completion of all things, including our lives, is in your powerful and gracious hands.

Give us the grace to accept our limitations and our weaknesses and our finiteness so that we might embrace our incompleteness as a fact of our lives and as a blessing rather than a curse.

And Lord, give us the courage not to accept our present state of incompleteness as the lot of our lives but rather to see that we can achieve, with your help, greater and greater completeness until we are, finally, in your presence, whole and complete and at rest.

Amen.

- TUESDAY 36 -
Co-Workers

We work with other people, and other people work with us. There are few if any careers that can be lived out and few if any jobs that can be done without the help of other people.

So bless our co-workers, Lord; bless those who work beside us or in conjunction with us. Also bless us as we are co-workers with our co-workers.

Help us to be true partners in our work; cause us to keep our common cause always before us. Keep whatever rivalry that comes with our work situation at a reasonable level; enable us to be happy for each other's success. Inspire us to be supportive of our co-workers when they have a difficult time; give us grace to take up each other's slack.

Whether or not we can truly be friends, cause us to have a healthy respect for one another; lead us to treat each other as human beings to be loved and never as objects to be used and manipulated.

Grant that we will share responsibility; cause us to share both in the credit when things go well and in the blame when they don't.

Thank you, Lord, for the privilege of having and of being co-workers. May our partnerships be healthy and productive and mutually supportive.

Amen.

- TUESDAY 37 -
Distractions

We are too easily distracted, and there are way too many distractions; it can be a devastating combination.

Thank you, Lord, for

a life so full of wonder,
a world so full of interesting things,
technology so full of information.

Help us, though, to be effective stewards of what is made available to us.

Help us not to be so distracted by the plethora of things—even good things—around us that we fail to focus on the people or on the tasks or on the moments that deserve the fullest attention we can give them.

If we must be distracted, let it be by something that merits our attention—something of great importance or great beauty or great need—more than that with which we are currently involved.

Guard us from the frivolous and wasteful shallowness of flitting from one thing to another and of never quite giving our full selves to who or what is before us.

Grant that we will invest ourselves in people and in projects that deserve our full attention.

And Lord, help us never to be distracted from that which should be the center of our lives all the time: loving you and loving other people.

Amen.

- TUESDAY 38 -

Question Mark

A question mark comes at the end of an interrogative sentence and thus marks that sentence as a request for information or for understanding or for clarification.

A question mark, then, helps to mark a sentence as a confession of our lack of knowledge or understanding or insight.

Question marks are evidence of our need for humility since they require us to submit ourselves to the knowledge or understanding of someone or something other than ourselves.

O God, we acknowledge the presence of many question marks in our lives; we acknowledge there is more we don't know and understand than we do know and understand.

We confess and repent of the sin of pride that sometimes keeps us from being submissive enough to ask about what we need to know.

Help us, O God, to celebrate the wonders of life and of the world and of the universe and of other people and of ourselves so that we might be appropriately and enthusiastically inquisitive.

Replace our frustrations over what we don't know with anticipation of and openness to what we can learn.

Some of our enduring and nagging questions are about you, God. Even as we acknowledge that we cannot comprehend you, we thank you for those sources of insight into your character with which you have in your grace provided us: the universe, the Bible, each other, and—especially—your Son Jesus Christ.

Bless us in our questioning, O God. Give us the drive to understand all we can and the grace to accept what we cannot.

Amen.

- TUESDAY 39 -

Basis

It is bad enough, O Lord, that we so often fail to take you into account;
that we so habitually and inexplicably fail to give you any thought at all;
that we so often fail to remember that you are.

It is even worse that we so often fail to live in utter gratitude for all you have done and are doing for us, the least of which is that you made us—for if you hadn't, we would not know the difference—and the greatest of which is that you save us—for if you didn't, we would know little or nothing other than the difference.

Forgive, O Lord, our inattention.
Forgive, O Lord, our ingratitude.

Help us to keep you always in the center of our thinking and feeling,
of our doing and acting, of our living and being.

And cause us always to be aware of and grateful for your many great acts
of deliverance and for the fact of our salvation.

Amen.

- TUESDAY 40 -

Life

It is a natural reflex for us to think of our lives as a gift from you that we do not want taken away from us or diminished.

We need to develop a conditioned reflex that will cause us to think of other people's lives as being the same kind of valuable gift that needs to be protected and enriched.

Except under the most extraordinary of circumstances we would never even think about taking someone's life from them.

But Lord, cause there to be growing within us a gracious and loving spirit that wants not only not to take life away but also to give life, a spirit that wants not only not to nurture hateful and vengeful and vindictive thoughts and feelings toward others but also to come to think of them as you think of them—as people to be loved so much that we would give up our lives for the sake of their lives and we would give up ourselves for the sake of their good.

Amen.

- TUESDAY 41 -
Away

Going away is an interesting process and a helpful experience.

When we go away from home, O Lord, lead us to places that will

cause us to grow in our knowledge of your world and of all your people,
provide us with opportunities to leave a mark that is positive and constructive,
give us chances to do some good in some way for someone,
remind us that—for others and for us—there's no place like home.

When we try to go away from you, O Lord, lead us to places where

our wandering will be in the long run productive,
our doubts will prove to be honest and necessary,
our sins will throw us back upon your grace,
our journey will result in our hearts wanting to rest in you.

Sometimes we go away or try to go away. Guard our spirits in the midst of our meandering. And always, always bring us back

to you—only to a fuller relationship with you,
to ourselves—only to a fuller knowledge of ourselves,
to our community—only to an expanded sense of community.

Amen.

- TUESDAY 42 -
Destinations

There are the places at which we plan to end up.
Then there are the places at which we do end up.

Sometimes they are the same. Oftentimes they are not.

Lord, help us to make the best plans we can using the best information we can and being guided by the best motivations we can so that we have a good chance to end up at the best destinations we can.

But keep us mindful that so much about where we end up has so much to do with the plans being made by other people who are using their own information and who are being guided by their own motivations.

In other words, Lord, guard us from being presumptive and arrogant.

At the same time, inspire us always to trust in your grace and mercy so that we can rest in the truth that, since our lives are ultimately in your hands, we will end up where you want us to be.

Amen.

- TUESDAY 43 -
Mediate

To mediate is to stand between two parties who are far apart and to try to bring them together. Help us, O Lord, to be mediators.

Insofar as we with your help can, enable us to be a source of peace-making between people around us in our workplace or our school or our home or our community or our church who are in conflict.

Help us also to be mediators between you and the people around us who are estranged from you; help us to be conduits of your grace and love to them even as we offer up prayers for them to you.

May our lives, O Lord, be so enlivened by your spirit and so covered in your grace that people around us will instinctively view us as contributors to the process of reconciliation.

Amen.

- TUESDAY 44 -

Laugh

Thank you, O God, for funny things, for things that make us laugh.

This life can be tough and hard and challenging, and so much of it is deadly serious; we need the relief that comedy and humor bring to us, and we thank you for the gift of laughter.

Help us to know and to practice the difference between laughing with one another and laughing at one another; give us the kind of hearts that are not willing to find inappropriate humor in someone's difference (as we perceive it) or in someone's misfortune.

Above all else, please give us the ability to laugh at ourselves, for in that ability we find ongoing hope for our continuing sanity.

May our laughter be an expression of our praise to you, O God, since your own sense of humor is quite evident not only in the duck-billed platypus but also in what we see when we look in the mirror.

Amen.

- TUESDAY 45 -

Rhyme

Poems sometimes rhyme—but not all the time (or) trees sway in perceptible synch.

Maybe we have to work a little harder and to think a little deeper to grasp the connections between the words of the ones that don't rhyme; the order and meaning of the words may not be obvious to us.

Sometimes we say of events that they have "no rhyme or reason," which is a way of saying they at first glance—and maybe at second or third or fourth glance—make no sense to us.

But that doesn't mean they don't make sense—at least they don't make sense to you, O God. And it doesn't mean that if we keep on looking and thinking and praying and living they won't come to make better sense to us.

And if they don't, well, that's where faith has to do its gracious work.

Moreover, even if a poem or an event seems at first glance to display rhyme and reason, that doesn't mean we have really gotten it.

O God, we thank you for those times in our lives when things seem to make sense even as we ask you not to let us always settle for the meaning we think we see at first glance.

And God, give us the faith we need to keep on moving and thinking and following and trusting in those times when there seems to be no rhyme or reason to it all; give us the patience to wait on you rather than to give in to the temptation to "make it fit."

Amen.

- TUESDAY 46 -
Dissent

The majority does not always get it right; going along with the crowd is not a good thing if you really think the crowd is headed over a cliff.

So sometimes, to be true to one's conscience and to one's principles—and even, although one must certainly be careful about such a claim, given how quick we are to equate what we think with what God must think, to God—one must offer a dissent to the prevailing opinion or attitude or to a contemplated action.

When the offering of such dissent is the right and even necessary thing to do, O Lord, give us the courage to offer it.

When we must offer such dissent, empower us to do so with Christian grace, love, and peace.

As we offer such dissent, help us to say just what we mean to say and not to say less than is required or more than is necessary.

And Lord, please help us to back up our words of dissent with appropriate acts of dissent, for if we can't or don't or won't put our actions where our words are, we can hardly assume that our hearts are in it; please deliver us from such hypocrisy.

Amen.

- TUESDAY 47 -
Noise

Quiet, when it comes, is a blessing readily recognized.
Noise, when it comes, is not usually so regarded.

Sometimes we need, for rest's sake, for prayer's sake, and for sanity's sake, to avoid the noise, to get away from the noise, and to shut out the noise—but not always. Because always attempting to shut out the noise is always trying to shut out life with all of its distractions, its irritations, its chaos, and its participants.

The noise reminds us that something is going on out there.

Lord, give us a proper perspective on and a healthy appreciation for the noise.

Use the noise to make and to keep us aware of the world in which we are to be involved with your hope and our help and of the people to whom we are to relate with your grace and our gifts.

Help us to shut out the noise enough to be healthy.
Help us to embrace the noise enough to be helpful.

Amen.

- TUESDAY 48 -
Cruciform

Please, O God, show me the way to live a cruciform life, a life shaped by my identification with the crucified Lord.

Please, O God, give me the grace and strength to grow a little every day in living such a life as you show me what it looks like.

It is, I believe and fear, the key to everything.

Amen.

- TUESDAY 49 -

Union

When we are born, we are born a body and a spirit; together,
those constitute our soul.

So long as we live here, our body and spirit never exist apart from one another; we experience life as the union of body and spirit that is our soul.

Yet we sense a divergence.

There comes a point at which our bodies begin their decline, their steady march toward our last breath after which our bodies return to dust.

That is not to say there will not be good health and continuing experiences of vitality; it is simply to admit that our bodies inevitably become older and weaker and finally they die.

The divergence comes because,

even as our bodies move into decline and toward death, our spirits can move into incline and toward life;

even as our bodies head in one direction, our spirits can by the grace of God move in another;

even as our bodies journey back to the earth from which they came, our spirits can journey back toward God from whom they came.

And then one day, thanks be to God for God's gift through Jesus Christ our Lord, there will be a great re-union of body and spirit we call resurrection.

Help us, O God, to live in full realization of our necessary divergence and in full expectation of the promised renewal and fulfillment of our union.

Amen.

- TUESDAY 50 -
Alongside

Fill us today with the constant awareness, O God, that you come alongside us and we walk alongside you as we travel along on our way and as we fulfill our responsibilities and as we rest at the end of the day.

After all, our presence with each other and our relationship with each other make all the difference in how we live as we travel along the way.

We have fellow travelers, other people who are also going down the road, and sometimes—maybe all the time—we need each other.

Fill us today with the constant awareness, O God, that there are others on the way with us and that we need to be ready and willing to come alongside them and to have them come alongside us.

After all, our presence with each other and our relationship with each other can make a real difference in how we live as we travel along the way.

Thank you, O God, for the grace of coming alongside; help us to grow in it.

Amen.

- TUESDAY 51 -
Missing

The holidays are wonderful, glorious, happy days—except when they're not.

One of the reasons is the experience of grief.

Some of us, O Lord, have very recently had loved ones to die. Some of us, O Lord, have not so recently but still since the last holiday season had loved ones to die.

Our grief is still raw.

Others of us, O Lord, long ago or even very long ago had loved ones to die.

Our grief is scabbed over but still present.

In some cases we have for whatever reasons not processed our grief as we should, and so we wear our grief like a death shroud of our own.

In other cases we have better processed our grief, but we may still at this time of year sense it even if we wear it more like a special occasion garment.

Help us, O Lord, with our missing those who are missing from us because they are missing from this life.

Help us, especially now but at all times, to know your grace, hope, and peace so that we might assimilate the lives of the missing to our lives in ways that produce health, wellness, and wholeness.

Help us always to know that Christmas means, among other things, Emmanuel—God is with us—which means you are with us in even our deepest losses, hurts, and griefs, and that in Christ you are working to make all things right and all things new.

May our blueness, if it must come, be at least tinged—if not covered—with joy.

Amen.

- TUESDAY 52 -
Always

O God,

you are with us—always;
you are beside us—always;
you are in us—always;
you are for us—always.

O God,

cause us to celebrate your presence—always;
cause us to follow your guidance—always;
cause us to echo your faithfulness—always;
cause us to live in your grace—always.

Always...

Amen.

Wednesday Prayers

- WEDNESDAY 1 -
Grace

I will need grace today, O Lord—

grace to remember that I am your beloved child,
grace to remember that they are your beloved children;

grace to know that all things work together,
grace to know that it is not my place to know how;

grace to be forgiven,
grace to forgive;

grace to trust,
grace to be trustworthy;

grace to know that nothing matters,
grace to know that everything matters;

grace to be of earth and of heaven,
grace to live so that at the end of the day it matters little in which I find myself.

Amen.

- WEDNESDAY 2 -
Reaction

O God, the people I will encounter today will be to me a varied lot, and I will instinctively react to them in varied ways. In fact, each one will be complicated and potentially confounding. Remind me that I will be like that to them, too; remind me that they might struggle to deal with me just like I might struggle to deal with them.

Give us the grace to extend grace to each other; give us the grace to accept grace from one another. For at the end of the day we are all in this together, and it is only by your grace that we can stay that way.

Amen.

- WEDNESDAY 3 -
Freedom

"Free from sin"
"Free from the law"
"Free in the Spirit"
"Free to choose"

"Free at last"

We are free! In Christ we are free!

"Freedom of worship"
"Freedom of assembly"
"Freedom of speech"
"Freedom of the press"

"Freedom"

We have freedom! In this land we are free!

Praise God! Thank the Lord!

Only help us, O Lord, to use our freedom

to do good rather than harm,
to heal rather than to hurt,
to build up rather than to tear down,
to bring together rather than to pull apart,
to embrace rather than to reject,
to accept responsibility rather than to evade responsibility.

And Lord, more than anything else, help us to use our freedom to show your love to everyone we can in every way we can.

In the name of the One who set us free,

Amen.

- WEDNESDAY 4 -
Earth

From the ground we are formed, says the Book, and to the ground we will return.

Open our eyes this day to our kinship with the earth,

to the truth that we are—both of us, this earth and we—at the same time strong and weak, enduring and fleeting, needed and needy;

to the truth that we can and do—both of us, this earth and we—sometimes help each other and sometimes hurt each other, the important difference being that while the earth's help or hurt are involuntary, ours are voluntary—we have a choice as to whether we will help or hurt.

Cause us this day to choose wisely and well, to help and not to hurt.

We give you praise, oh God, for this good and beautiful world in which we live. Help us to be wise and faithful and loving caretakers of it.

Amen.

- WEDNESDAY 5 -
Others

The living of this day will involve living with others, O Lord,

some with whom we are intimately involved,
some with whom we are barely acquainted,
some with whom we are partners in vocation,
some with whom we are friends online,
some with whom we are friends in person,
some with whom we are friends indeed,
some from whom we are sadly estranged,
some to whom we are currently strangers,
some by whom we are potentially threatened,
some by whom we are perpetually blessed.

Help us, O Lord, in our dealings with them all to remember that we stand in those same relationships to them; that, while we hope and pray they will be loving and kind and honest and open and vulnerable and caring and redemptive toward us, we have no control over them; but that we do have a lot to do with how we will be toward them.

So Lord, please help us to be loving and kind and honest and open and vulnerable and caring and redemptive toward those with whom the living of this day will involve living—for their sake, for our sake, and for Christ's sake.

Amen.

- WEDNESDAY 6 -
Enough

Sometimes we want too much, Lord.

We want no trouble in our lives.
We want everyone to like us.
We want all decisions to be easy.
We want every choice to be clear-cut.
We want everything to be all right—

right here,
right now.

It can't be like that, we know, but we are bad to want what we can't have.

Help us this day to want what we can have, to want what is better anyway, to want not too much but just enough. Help us to want

to know we are your children,
to know you love us,
to know we are forgiven,
to know we are in Christ,
to know, in a way that goes far below the surface and far beyond the obvious, that everything is all right—

right here,
right now.

Amen.

- WEDNESDAY 7 -

One

There may be, I am told

as many as 140 billion galaxies in the universe,
of which our Milky Way is one;

as many as 400 billion stars in the Milky Way,
of which our sun is one;

as many as 10 billion trillion planets in the universe,
of which our earth is one.

I am but one person on that one planet.

My Bible says you care for me—that even the hairs on my head are numbered—and you love me—that nothing can separate me from the love of God in Christ Jesus our Lord.

Help me, O Lord, when I start to feel lost and overwhelmed and forgotten, to remember your care and your love and to rest in you.

Amen.

- WEDNESDAY 8 -

Turning

To repent is to turn. Lord, you know and we know that we need to repent, to turn.

In some ways we need to make a 180° turn because we're just plain going the wrong way and the only solution is to turn completely around and head in the opposite direction.

So help us, Lord, to turn our backs on what needs to be turned away from and to turn our faces toward the better way you have for us.

Those are obvious to us.

But in some ways we need to make a smaller turn, maybe 90° or 45° or 10° or 3° or 1°—perhaps just the very slightest turn but an important turn nonetheless.

Those are less obvious to us.

So help us, Lord, to make those small turns, those small adjustments, those slight turnings away from self and toward you and toward others, that just might make the difference between a tolerable or even a good life and an abundant one.

Amen.

- WEDNESDAY 9 -
Remember

When things become difficult today—

when the next problem is one too many,
when the next person is a burden rather than a joy,
when the next effort to help myself is no help at all,
when the next turning inward turns into a turning downward—

help me, O Lord, to remember you.

Help me to remember

your love,
your grace,
your mercy,
your faithfulness,
your presence.

And in remembering, cause me to turn upward to you—our Father in heaven—so that I can turn inward to you—O Holy Spirit in me—and so that I can turn outward to you—the body of Christ in the world.

Amen

- WEDNESDAY 10 -
Thirsty

"I thirst," Jesus said as he hung on the cross; it was the thirst of death he was experiencing. We get thirsty, too, so thirsty sometimes that it feels like we're dying of it—

thirsty for wholeness,
thirsty for justice,
thirsty for integrity,
thirsty for forgiveness,
thirsty for love,
thirsty for grace—
thirsty mainly for you.

Cause us, Lord, to turn regularly and often—perpetually—to Jesus who said, after all, that he is the living water, the water in whom is life.

Cause us, Lord, to remember that other people are thirsty, too, so that we will offer them—and even be to them—a cup of cool water in Jesus' name.

Amen.

- WEDNESDAY 11 -
Guidance

It is difficult to offer guidance to someone, even when, so far as we can tell, our hearts are in the right place and our motives are based in a genuine desire to help.

Sometimes, though, we need to accept the responsibility that is ours because of the grace with which you have gifted us and because of the need of the one whom you have placed before us.

So Lord, help us to share graciously of the grace you have given us, and may that sharing come from a genuine humility that will help lead to a growth in grace and humility for the brother or sister to whom we are relating in that difficult moment.

Bless us all with the ability to exercise the faith you have given us so that we can think rationally and not grandiosely or belittlingly about ourselves, whether we are the one giving or receiving the guidance.

Amen.

- WEDNESDAY 12 -
Sharing

Deliver us, O Lord, from death by oxymoron:

"Selfish Christian"
"Greedy disciple"
"Hard-hearted believer"
"Graceless recipient of grace."

Forgive us when we take your good gifts—be they spiritual or physical
—and cling to them protectively, as if to let them go is to lose them,
when in fact to let them go is to gain them and even to multiply them.

Cause us to remember—and having remembered, to live in light of it
—that while charity begins at home and that while, Cain's legacy notwithstanding,
we are our brother's and sister's keeper; there is no such thing as someone who is
not our neighbor.

Thank you, Lord, for the privilege of sharing and for the grace of giving.

May our opportunities and our willingness increase.

Amen.

- WEDNESDAY 13 -
Good and Evil

First, Lord, we ask for the ability to know what evil is so that we might avoid it and
oppose it.

Sometimes it's obvious, of course.

But sometimes what seems obviously evil to us seems that way because of our biases
or opinions or other assumptions.

Sometimes we think evil is what someone else does that we don't like—
or what someone we don't like does.

Sometimes we think something that is evil is not because it works to our benefit or because it is easier not to rock the boat.

So, Lord, where our definition of evil needs to be narrowed, narrow it;
where it needs to be broadened, broaden it.

Second, Lord, we ask for the ability to know what good is so that we might practice it and support it.

Sometimes it's obvious, of course.

But sometimes what seems obviously good to us seems that way because of our biases or opinions or other assumptions.

Sometimes we think good is what we do because we like to do it—
or what people we like do.

Sometimes we think something that is not good is because it works to our benefit or because it maintains the status quo.

So, Lord, where our definition of good needs to be narrowed, narrow it;
where it needs to be broadened, broaden it.

Help us to know and to do and to support that which is based in and grows out of the kind of love and grace and mercy we see in Christ our Lord, because such is surely the ultimate definition of good.

Amen.

- WEDNESDAY 14 -

Alive

A cat has nine lives, so they say, while a person has only one.

Looking back, though, I feel like I've used up at least ten;
that I've dodged death more times than I can remember.

Thank you, God, for your protection, for the fact that thus far neither circumstance nor sin nor foolishness have done me in.

Looking back at all the times that could have been my time but weren't helps me to trust that when the time comes that is my time, it will be the right time.

In that is peace.
In that is praise.

Meanwhile, I thank you that I am alive.
Help me to live like it.

Amen.

- WEDNESDAY 15 -

Sick

Bless the sick, O Lord.

Bless those who are dealing with

passing illness,
chronic illness,
serious illness, or
terminal illness.

Bless those who are dealing with their illness

in a hospital,
in a nursing facility, or
at home.

Bless those who are dealing with their illness

in community or
in isolation.

We ask for their healing.

We also ask that they will know your grace

so they can experience your presence even in the worst of it,
so they can know wholeness even in the brokenness of it,
so they can see some purpose and meaning in all of it.

Thank you, Lord, for your blessings on the sick.

Amen.

- WEDNESDAY 16 -
Weight

Sometimes I feel like the weight of the world is on my shoulders. It is not; it is on yours. That is good because you can handle it and I cannot.

Lord, please forgive the pride that causes me to take on more than is mine.

Sometimes I want to lay down the lesser weights that are appropriately mine.

I cannot; they are mine.

That is good because they give me purpose and meaning.

Lord, please forgive the ingratitude that causes me to want to lay down what I should carry.

Help me, Lord, to live this day and all days in full partnership with you, in full awareness and acceptance of the fact that we are in this together and that even my part, which I must do, is—when all is said and done—on your strong shoulders—because that is where I stand.

Amen.

- WEDNESDAY 17 -
God

It is to you, O God, we pray. But how much thought do we actually give to you?

How much do we ponder the wonder of the fact that you, the maker and sustainer and redeemer of all that is, allow and even encourage us to enter into conversation and into relationship with you?

Thank you, God.

To think about you analytically and to talk about you descriptively only get us so far, though, because we cannot fully understand or describe you.

Forgive us for the folly of acting like we can.

Your essence seems to be given in two lines from your Book:

God is love.
God was in Christ reconciling the world unto himself.

Our response to you, then, should be to love you and other people and to work toward reconciliation.

So help us, O God, to live as a response to who you have revealed yourself to be.

Amen.

- WEDNESDAY 18 -
Take/Receive

Guard us today, Lord, from being takers. Guard us from

an attitude of greed,
a sense of entitlement, and
a spirit of selfishness

that keep us focused on what we can take for ourselves rather than on what we can give for others.

At the same time, Lord, help us to be receivers. Give us

an attitude of graciousness,
a sense of need, and
a spirit of openness

that will enable us to know we can't fill all of our gaps by ourselves and that we are incomplete without the love and grace and help of others.

Guard us from the gracelessness of taking.

Give us the grace of receiving.

Amen.

- WEDNESDAY 19 -
Progress

Sometimes what we call progress does not deserve the name, because moving forward in the wrong direction is not helpful.

Help us, Lord, to move forward in the right directions.

Help us to make progress in

our commitment to you,
our commitment to one another,
our trust in you,
our embrace of life,
our participation in eternal life,
our exercise of grace,
our offering of peace,
our giving of ourselves.

Sometimes we will, as we try to make progress, find ourselves taking one step forward and two steps backward. When that happens, Lord, please encourage us with the possibility that a little regress on the right road is better than a lot of progress on the wrong one.

Amen.

- WEDNESDAY 20 -

Maybe

Today, like all days, will be full of questions to which we must respond.

Help us, Lord, to say "Maybe" to those questions that merit an ambiguous answer.

Sometimes
until we can gather more information,
we should say "Maybe."

Sometimes
until we can pray some more,
we should say "Maybe."

Sometimes
until we can determine what is good and what is best,
we should say "Maybe."

Sometimes
until we understand the relationship between the truth and our opinion,
we should say "Maybe."

Sometimes
until we have considered the impact of a commitment on our witness,
we should say "Maybe."

Sometimes
until greater light has penetrated our darkness,
we should say "Maybe."

Often we need the humility to know what we don't know and the patience to wait until we know more of what we need to know.

There are many questions to which we should say "Maybe" on this day and on all days.

Help us, Lord, to say "Maybe."

Amen.

- WEDNESDAY 21 -

If

"If" is a powerful little word because it places us in the realm of possibility.

"If I do this thing, what might happen?"
"If I decide in this way, what might be the result?"
"If I say these words, what might be the effect?"
"If I follow this path, what might be the outcome?"

We ponder the possibilities and then we imagine the desired outcome and then we muster the courage and the hope to take the plunge.

Or sometimes we ponder the possibilities and then we imagine the desired outcome and then we give in to fear and submit to paralysis.

O God, may the "ifs" that confront us inspire in us excitement over the possibilities, hope in the future, and faith in your guidance.

And may our awareness of the fact that we cannot know the outcome in advance not condemn us to the limbo of inertia.

Amen.

- WEDNESDAY 22-

Belief

I can choose to believe the moon is made of cheese or the earth is flat but my belief, as convinced as I may be in it, does not make it so.

All the belief in the world can't change the facts.

On the other hand, not everything that is true because it is real can be verified in ways that will satisfy someone who must have "proof"—and whether or not we believe in some such things can make all the difference.

So Lord, we believe—in love, in mercy, in grace, in peace, in heaven, in resurrection, and in you. Please help our unbelief.

Amen.

- WEDNESDAY 23 -
Hints

It would be nice, I guess, to get the occasional burning bush or chariot of fire or wet/dry fleece, but I'm not holding my breath. Besides, the hints are enough:

the baby's smile,
the old couple's devotion,
the uncomfortable shift,
the strangely warmed heart,
the gentle prompt,
the comforting presence,
the disturbing awareness,
the sense of more,
the pull upward.

Yes, the hints are enough if we will only pay attention.

Help us, O God, to pay attention to the hints in which we hear your still small voice.

Amen.

- WEDNESDAY 24 -
Numb

It is tempting to seek numbness; after all, there is so much in us and around us to stimulate us that it can get oppressive sometimes—and we feel the need for relief. Such a desire can be unhealthy, though, if it turns into a persistent desire to escape life or to avoid reality.

Lord cause us to embrace our lives and not to flee them. Help us to live to the fullest and to incorporate our experiences in ways that will help make us more whole.

And Lord, when we do take a break or when we do seek relief, help us to avoid those ways of escaping that numb us. Help us rather to seek ways of renewal in which we can find true refreshment and re-creation.

Help us not to seek numbness.
Help us to seek rest in you.

Amen.

- WEDNESDAY 25 -

Trust

To trust someone is to count on her or him to be there and to be dependable.

We are blessed if we have people in our lives who have proven worthy of our trust. At their best they are not perfect, we know, but if they have a heart that causes them to prefer the worst pain imaginable to the pain of letting us down, we are blessed.

So thank you, Lord, for the trustworthy people in our lives.
Help us to be trustworthy, too.

At the same time, help us, Lord, to put our full and utter trust in you, for you are absolutely trustworthy and dependable and faithful and, while the trustworthy people in our lives will see us through to the end, you are the only One who can see us through—not only to the end but beyond it.

With every step we take today, O Lord, increase our trust in you.

Amen.

- WEDNESDAY 26 -

Zeal

Give us zeal, Lord—
a passion that comes from caring deeply about something that matters greatly to us.

But protect us from misguided zeal—
a passion motivated by ways of thinking and living that are not worthy of those whose lives are being formed in the image of Christ: prejudice, greed, envy, anger, fear, insecurity, or bigotry, for example.

Fill us instead with worthy zeal—
a passion motivated by ways of thinking and living that are worthy of those who love you, who follow Jesus, and who are guided by your Spirit: grace, mercy, faith, peace, justice, and love, for example.

Give us zeal, Lord—
a passion that causes us to care about matters and situations and predicaments about which you care. Then, inspire us to do what we can to address such matters and situations and predicaments.

Amen.

- WEDNESDAY 27 -
Stumble

Sometimes, Lord, we stumble.

Protect us from the self-delusion that insists we didn't stumble when we did.

Forgive us for the stumbles that come because of wrong choices we make or wrong paths we take or wrong motives we nourish.

Give us grace and strength when we stumble to get up one more time.

And guard us from a fear of stumbling that would prevent us from walking ahead boldly in the living of our lives.

Amen.

- WEDNESDAY 28 -
Rise

O God,

When we are knocked down by life's circumstances,
cause us to rise!

When we are at ease and you put into our hearts something that needs to be done,
cause us to rise!

When we are pressed down by sorrow over the predicament of another,
cause us to rise!

When we are beset by sloth when we need to be about your business,
cause us to rise!

When we are confronted with the realities of oppression, hate, fear, and prejudice,
cause us to rise!

And when we are lying in our graves and the great day of the Lord's return comes,
cause us to rise!

We pray in the name of the One who is risen,

Amen!

- WEDNESDAY 29 -
Three

There is one God.

That one God is God in three persons—the blessed Trinity.

So we have tried to describe the indescribable; so we have tried to fathom the unfathomable.

God, so you have revealed yourself to us.

But you also have revealed yourself to us as love: "God is love," your Book says.

The fact that you are love gives us one way to think about your "threeness" that is helpful. If one is to love, after all, one must have someone to love. So maybe your nature as Father, Son, and Holy Spirit at least shows that being in relationship is basic to who you are.

This much we know: in your grace you allow your children to love you, and in your grace you empower us to love each other.

O God, grant that the kind of love that is basic to who you are will also be basic to who we are.

Amen.

- WEDNESDAY 30 -
World

It's a big world and lots of people live in it—and this nation is different than that nation, and this group is different than that group, and this person is different than that person.

On the one hand, we can't help but see things from our own limited perspective and in light of our own limited experience.

On the other hand, it will be a better—a more peaceable—world if we try harder to understand the perspective and the experiences of others.

O God, we thank you for our little place in the world and for the privilege we have to live in it and through it.

We thank you also for the great variety of people and cultures and traditions that flourish in our world.

Help us to get together.

And when we do get together, help us really to be together; to relate to each other with respect and love and understanding.

Amen.

- WEDNESDAY 31 -
Return

It's good to get away; it's also good to get back.

When you leave, all you can think about is what you're getting away from: stress, frustration, and routine—to name a few things you don't miss.

But the truth is, there is so much to get back to: family, friends, home, pets, productive work, and routine—to name a few things you do miss.

Thank you, Lord, for the gift of leaving.
Thank you, Lord, for the gift of returning.

In the place where those gifts touch, may we find more peace and hope than we had before receiving them.

Amen.

- WEDNESDAY 32 -
Pressure

All of us are under pressure; the amount and the type vary from person to person, from situation to situation, and from day to day.

Pressure can flatten us.

Pressure can bear down on something until it is flattened; it can have the same effect on us. In our case, such flattening can be a negative thing—we can be laid out or laid low—or it can be a positive thing—in a flattened state we may be more ready to look up to God for help and to be shaped by God.

Pressure can force us.

Pressure can bear down on something until what is inside it is forced out—think of a toothpaste tube or a geyser, for examples—it can have the same effect on us. Under pressure what is inside us can be forced to come out, whether it's faith or lack of faith, love or lack of love, hope or lack of hope, or grace or lack of grace.

Pressure can form us.

Pressure can bear down on something until it is formed into smaller parts or until it is formed into something more valuable and enduring. So pressure might pulverize a mineral or it might cause materials to turn to diamond. In the same way, pressure can break or make us.

O God, we confess the pressure under which we live. We ask that we will be open to your grace and love so that the pressure will work in us to do helpful and positive things rather than hurtful and negative things.

May the pressure we are under flatten us so that we can in trust be used by you; may it force us to show who we really are; and may it form us into people of beauty and value for the sake of your kingdom.

Amen.

- WEDNESDAY 33 -

Roles

We have our roles to play:

father,
mother,
sister,
brother,
wife,
husband,
butcher,
baker,
candlestick maker.

We have personal and family roles to play, and we have vocational roles to play.

To play a role can be very fulfilling,
if it is a role we were born to play.

To play a role can be very frustrating.
if it is a role we are only acting out rather than living out.

The truth is, it's a good life if we can with honesty and integrity fill our roles most of the time and if we can still be faithful and diligent the rest of the time.

Lord, give us roles in life that match our gifts and talents.

Lord, thank you for the fulfillment we find in the good days;
grant us patience and perseverance on the other days.

Lord, help us to do good to others as we live out our roles; help us to be as concerned—if not more concerned—about how we can help others be happy as we are about our own happiness.

And Lord, in whatever role we find ourselves, enable us to glorify you by serving you and by serving others.

Amen.

- WEDNESDAY 34 -
Single-Mindedness

We have way too much on our minds.

There are all the concerns that grow out of daily living. So we think about our families, our jobs, our friends, our enemies, our finances, our houses, our yards, and our health—not to mention what to have for dinner tonight and what to watch on TV.

On top of all that, we can—thanks to the twenty-four-hour news cycle—think just as much as we want (and probably much more than we want) about just about everything going on with just about everyone just about everywhere.

It is no wonder we are driven to distraction and then right on past distraction to confusion.

So it might appear ludicrous to pray for single-mindedness, for the ability to focus on only one thing, for clarity that brings order to our thinking and to our living.

Nevertheless, O Lord, give us such single-mindedness, such focus, and such clarity.

We don't ask that all our concerns go away.

We do ask that our devotion to, our love for, and our following of our Lord Jesus Christ will be for us the only thing so that all the other things will take their rightful places as a piece of that only thing.

Grant us single-mindedness, O Lord.

Amen.

- WEDNESDAY 35 -
Providence

One ground of our hope is an awareness that God is working God's purposes out in and through the universe and in and through us.

Some would call such an "awareness" a delusion, a self-deception that amounts to a coping mechanism and a survival tool.

All I and many, many others know is that it feels like a fact of life to us.

Thank you, God, for what your Word teaches us about your commitment to working your purposes out.

Thank you, God, for the ability to look back over our lives and to see your guidance and your grace.

Thank you, God, for the assurance communicated to us by your Spirit and by our experiences.

May our hope grow today in the light of who you are and what you are doing.

Amen.

- WEDNESDAY 36 -
Authority

Everyone in the world has at least one other someone who has authority over them—and most of us have many.

Sometimes someone has authority over us because of the way things are set up for the sake of having order rather than chaos: bosses over employees, law enforcement officers over the general populace, military officers over enlisted personnel, teachers over students, parents over children, coaches over players, and so on.

Sometimes someone has authority over us because we have out of conviction or principle chosen to submit ourselves to another, such as when followers of Christ heed Paul's instruction to "submit yourselves to one another out of reverence for Christ" in our marital relationships or our church relationships or our other relationships.

Bless, O God, those in authority over us and us in our authority over others. Make us wise in our deliberations and in our decisions as we exercise our authority; make us compassionate and gracious in our attitudes and actions toward those under our authority; make us humble in the application of our authority.

Bless us, O God, in our submission to those in authority over us. Make our submission a gracious submission so that we might be kept from jealousy and bitterness; make our submission a bold submission so that we will be willing to speak necessary truths to those in authority over us; make our submission a discerning submission so that we will know when and how to resist an authority whose will goes against your will so drastically that it must be resisted.

Authority comes from you, O God. Cause us to see it as a gift.

At the same time, we receive this and all your gifts in imperfect vessels. So cause us to exercise our authority and to submit to authority graciously and wisely.

And cause us always to reserve our ultimate submission for the highest Authority.

Amen.

- WEDNESDAY 37 -
Faces

We see someone face-to-face, we say, by which we mean we have a personal encounter that has some sense of intimacy to it rather than a long-distance encounter by telephone or internet that doesn't.

In our society hardly anyone veils their face, so in a way we are wide open to one another.

We aren't really, though, because we wear all kinds of internal masks to try to hide our true selves from one another and from ourselves and even—we think in our silliness—from you, O God.

Still, our faces tell the tale of our lives.

When we look in the mirror we see our history reflected back at us in the sparkle or dullness of our eyes, in the lines and creases on our skin, and in the upward or downward turn of the corners of our mouth.

So when we are looking each other in the face, when we are really looking each other in the face—and how often do we really do that?—we are gazing into each other's lives, into each other's experiences and histories.

O Lord, teach us to take our own faces seriously, to take ourselves seriously; teach us to, as is appropriate, celebrate or repent of—but in all cases to accept—those aspects of our living that have marked our faces as they have.

And Lord, teach us to take the faces of others seriously, to take their lives seriously; teach us to take the time and to make the effort to have real encounters with others, to know and to be known by them, to love and to be loved by them.

Help us, when we see a face, really to see that face.

Amen.

- WEDNESDAY 38 -
Comma

A comma provides a break in a sentence.

Used correctly, a comma breaks the flow of a sentence so as to make its reading a more effective and even pleasant experience.

Used incorrectly, a comma, breaks the flow of a sentence, so as to make its reading, a less effective, and unpleasant, experience.

Lord, we need commas in our lives. We need breaks and pauses that will serve the healthy purposes of letting us catch our breath and organize our thoughts.

Help us to insert them at the right places.

But there is an art to the proper use of commas, and there is a discipline to the avoidance of their misuse and especially their overuse.

So Lord, teach us not to put breaks and pauses where they don't belong in our lives; teach us not to interrupt the creative stream of our lives with untimely and unhelpful diversions.

There are breaks and pauses that increase our ability to focus, and there are breaks and pauses that decrease our ability to focus. Help us to know and to practice the difference.

Amen.

- WEDNESDAY 39 -
God Alone

We tend, O Lord, to be theoretical monotheists but practical polytheists. We claim and say there is only one God, but we think and act as if there are many.

Forgive us, Lord, for ascribing ultimate importance or for giving our ultimate allegiance to anyone or anything other than you.

Help us to increase in maturity and wholeness so that our hearts, minds, and lives will more and more will one thing: to love you to the point that you are everything and that any other thing in our lives is for us a part of the one thing of loving you.

Make us mindful of those people or institutions or positions or possessions to which we ascribe too much authority and in which we have tried to find too much security.

Where necessary, cause us to walk away from them completely.

Where necessary, cause us to keep them but to see them for what they are and for what they aren't.

We confess that you and you alone are God.

May our attitude, our bearing, our thoughts, our allegiances, our relationships, our actions, our feelings—may everything we are and do—reveal the integrity of our confession.

Amen.

- WEDNESDAY 40 -
Marriage

Some people view marriage as limiting, stifling, and unfulfilling.
Some people experience marriage as limiting, stifling, and unfulfilling.

That's unfortunate, O God, since you intend for marriage to be liberating and fulfilling and so full of possibilities that we would never exhaust them all if we worked at it all the time—which we should.

We thank you, God,

for each other;
for the most intimate relationship we will ever have;
for the closest relationship into which we will ever voluntarily enter;
for the covenant we have with you that allows us to live in great trust;
for the wonder of knowing another so fully and so freely.

Constantly remind us and keep us aware, O God, of the many aspects of our relationship—physical, emotional, mental, and spiritual—that can and should be willingly and wonderingly and gratefully and excitedly explored and developed and honed and appreciated and celebrated.

If our minds and our hearts and our bodies and our homes are continuously and purposely being filled up with the miracle of each other and the miracle of us, then there will be no room in our minds or hearts or bodies or homes for another.

In that is great joy.

Amen.

- WEDNESDAY 41 -
Fire

Fire is a constructive thing; it offers heat and light and comfort.

Fire is also a destructive thing; it consumes and devastates.

So many of the realities in our world and in our lives are like fire; they can do good or they can do harm, depending on how they are used and particularly on how they are or are not controlled.

O God, we have fire in our bodies and in our spirits and in our minds—passions, desires, and drives. Help us to channel and to use them in ways that will be for our good and for the good of others.

O God, we have fire in our cultures and in our politics and in our science and in our churches—undeveloped potential, partially understood truths, and unexamined assumptions. Help us to stoke the fires that will lead us to glorify you and to help our fragile world, and help us to quench the fires that would lead us to break your heart and to devastate one another.

May our fires be fanned or extinguished according to your wisdom and will.

Amen.

- WEDNESDAY 42 -
Differences

Thank you, Lord, that this is not a boring world. Thank you for the great diversity in the world that makes it such an interesting place to live.

When we travel to other places we see different flora and fauna and are amazed in the differences we find.

Cause us to be especially thankful for the differences in people; not only are there cultural differences between groups of people, but also there are personality differences in each individual.

Forgive us when we want everyone to be like us or when we think it would be a better world if everyone could be like us.

Help us instead to celebrate the great diversity you have instilled in your human creation.

Help us to celebrate those differences that mark our humanity.

Amen.

- WEDNESDAY 43 -

Politick

To "politick" is to participate in discussions or activities of a political nature.

Lord, pour your grace out on those of us who politick professionally;
guard their hearts and words and attitudes so that they might maintain their integrity—and deliver those who have already or long ago lost it.

Lord, pour your grace out on those of us who politick non-professionally;
guard our hearts and words and attitudes so that we might maintain our perspective—and deliver those who have already or long ago lost it.

Cause us all, in our political stances and discussions and actions, to seek and to speak the truth.

Prevent us from selling out to a particular system so that we cease thinking for ourselves.

Help us never to give in to fear or despair or anger that clouds our judgment and turns us from a legitimate and basic trust in you.

When we politick, O Lord, lead us to do so in a way that brings glory to you, good to our community, and grace to all.

Amen.

- WEDNESDAY 44 -

Cry

Thank you, O God, for the ability to cry. Thank you for the capacity to have our hearts broken and to feel pain and to experience suffering.

To lack such ability and such capacities would mean we are not fully human, and so to be thankful for these lives of ours means we are thankful even for the aspects of those lives that bring pain to our souls and tears to our eyes.

It doesn't take much sensitivity, though, for us to cry over the events and experiences and feelings that cause us personal pain. We can cry over such things and still be selfish; we can respond with sensitivity to personal losses and still be insensitive to the suffering others are experiencing.

O God, soften our hearts so that they will break over the brokenness of others; give us the grace to cry over that which brings tears to their eyes.

O God, attune our hearts to your heart so that our hearts will break over the situations and conditions in the lives of people that cause your heart to break; give us the grace to cry over that which brings tears to your eyes.

Then dry our tears and give us clear vision so that we might see our own lives and the lives of others as you see those lives and then, by your strength, do what we can to help make things better.

Amen.

- WEDNESDAY 45 -
Finite

There are limits to what we can do.

Lord, give us the wisdom, humility, and rationality to accept that truth; we will have much more peace and much less pressure if we do.

Help us to celebrate and to enjoy our finiteness.

On the other hand, we are usually capable of pressing out toward our limits more than we customarily do.

Lord, give us the incentive and the courage to push our limits; inspire us to hone our talents and to develop our abilities and to live in ways that make the most of these admittedly limited but still wondrous and too often untapped or underdeveloped capabilities with which you have gifted us.

Help us to celebrate and to enjoy our finiteness.

Amen.

- WEDNESDAY 46 -

Assent

Sometimes we assent to an attitude or an assertion or an action by what we say: "Yes, that's right" or "I agree" or "Amen."

Sometimes we assent to an attitude or an assertion or an action by what we don't say; since we don't dissent, our silence is taken as assent.

Develop in us integrity so that our "Yes" will be clearly "Yes" and our "No" will be clearly "No."

Develop in us wisdom so that we will give our assent to that which builds up and not to that which tears down, to that which promotes love and not to that which promotes hate, and to that which fosters community and not to that which fosters division.

Develop in us discernment so that we will give our assent to what matters to you.

Develop in us wholeness so that our actions will demonstrate our agreement with those motives, attitudes, ideas, and principles to which we assent with our thoughts and our words.

Amen.

- WEDNESDAY 47 -

Silence

O God,

the silence should be centering
because there is no one in the silence except for you and me;

the silence should be calming
because there is no noise in the silence to disturb my peace;

the silence should be clarifying
because there are no thoughts in the silence but the ones I think.

But,

the truth is that to the silence I bring everyone I know and everyone I have known;
the truth is that to the silence I bring all the noise of my day and of my life;
the truth is that to the silence I bring the thoughts expressed by others and the thoughts I imagine others would express.

So,

I need in the silence a stronger sense of your presence
to crowd out the other people;

I need in the silence a stronger sense of your peace
to turn down the noise;

I need in the silence a stronger sense of your unconditional love
to drive out my concerns about what people think of me.

Thank you, O God, for the silence. When I am in it, help me to be fully present to you even as you are willing to be fully present to me. Remind me in the silence that I am your beloved child.

Amen.

- WEDNESDAY 48 -
Refuge

Before I start praying that you will be my refuge, O God, remind me that you are my refuge.

You are my refuge in the sense that you are a fortress to which I will retreat when I am wounded or exhausted or in trouble or under attack and just generally on the run from whomever and whatever and anything and everything, and in the sense that you are a fortress from which I will, after I have been healed or refreshed or rescued or delivered or welcomed, go back out into the world ready to try again to be faithful in the face of whomever and whatever and anything and everything.

So rather than pray that you will be my refuge, O God, I pray that you will never let me forget that you are my refuge, the fortress to which I come in and from which I go out.

Amen.

- WEDNESDAY 49 -
Companions

Thank you, Lord, that we are not alone; thank you that we do not walk this always challenging road by ourselves.

Thank you for our sisters and brothers, our partners in faith, those who struggle like we do but who are there when we need a hand to steady us or to hold us or to push us.

Thank you for our brothers and sisters all over the world, for the millions of companions we don't know and who don't know us but pray for us.

Thank you for the Holy Spirit who is always with us to comfort, to counsel, to convict, to encourage, to empower, to teach, to lead, to challenge, and to guide us.

Thank you for our companions on the way; remind us that we never walk alone.

Give us grace to be good, faithful, and dependable companions in return.

Amen.

- WEDNESDAY 50 -
Lines

At all times of the year, but even more at this time of the year, we find ourselves standing in lines.

Thank you, God, for the privilege of standing in a line with other people because such standing teaches us some valuable lessons; help us to learn them well.

Help us to learn of patience.

Teach us how to wait graciously; after all, we must always wait for the coming of your Son, for the formation of our lives into your image, and for our arrival at our ultimate destination. So teach us to show grace in our waiting for little things so that we might have more grace in our waiting for big things.

Help us to learn of equality.

A line is a great equalizer; there we are not rich or poor, black or white or brown, Jew or Catholic or Protestant—we are just in line. When we wait in line, we wait in line with other people and we are all in the same predicament; we are all in it together in our waiting. Teach us to look at each other and, in looking, to pray for each other. Give us some understanding of and some appreciation for each other. Grow hearts within us that inspire us to be, with great kindness, good to one another.

Thank you, God, for the opportunities to learn of and to grow in our humanity as we stand in line with other human beings. Help us to learn our lessons well.

Amen.

- WEDNESDAY 51 -
Poets

Thank you, God, for poets, for people who by gift and by practice can see to the heart of things and who can through the use of well-chosen and well-said words help us to see what life means both within and beyond the mundane.

Give even to those of us who will never write a word of poetry something of the heart and insight of a poet so that we might be able to sense, to hear, to see, and to know what events and words and people really are and really mean.

Advent and Christmas and other such times call especially for poets
—but really, all times do.

Form in us hearts that are sensitive to the poetry of it all.

Amen.

- WEDNESDAY 52 -
Conspire

To conspire is to be together and to get together on a matter so as to do something about it; conspiracies often exist in secret, whether they are just below the surface or are deeply hidden.

Help us to be more conspiratorial, O God; help us to be more involved in what you are doing—sometimes beneath the surface and sometimes out in the open—to stir up revolution and to bring in your kingdom.

Lead us to be more involved in your conspiracy to make all things right through the ways shown by Jesus, who is the model, inspiration, and leader of your great conspiracy.

Empower us to be involved in your conspiracy of grace, of love, of mercy, of peace, of kindness, of forgiveness, of suffering, and of sacrifice.

Grant us insight so that the conspiracy with which we are involved and to which we are dedicated is yours and not ours.

Amen.

Thursday Prayers

- THURSDAY 1 -
Steps

Guide my steps, O Lord, this day.

Sometimes I will step backwards, trying to retreat or to escape, driven back by guilt or pushed back by fear or compelled back by failure or nudged back by fatigue, perhaps fleeing the light that reveals more of the way forward than I want to accept or that reveals more of me than I want to face, maybe preferring the darkness to the light. When I step backwards, O Lord, guide my steps, whether or not I can see my way clearly.

Sometimes I will stand still, trying to comprehend where I am, attempting to understand how I got there, perhaps unsure which way to go, maybe afraid to go any way at all, at times needing the courage to step into the darkness, at other times needing the strength to step into the light. When I stand still, O Lord, guide my steps, whether or not I can see my way clearly.

Sometimes I will move forward, trying to find my way, groping in the darkness, trying to follow the light that at times seems so very dim, or trying to avoid the light that at times seems so very bright. When I move forward, O Lord, guide my steps, whether or not I can see my way clearly.

Guide my steps, O Lord, this day.

Amen.

- THURSDAY 2 -
Whatever

O Lord,

I do not know what this day holds; I do not know what lies out there ready to erupt or to trickle or to continue trickling into my life—

what joys,
what sorrows,
what successes,
what failures,
what revelations,

what doubts,
what questions,
what answers,
what opportunities,
what developments,
what beginnings,
what endings.

Whatever is to come, Lord,

I will praise you;
I will trust you;
I will rest in you;
I will follow you;
I will submit to you;
I will love you;
I will love others.

Those are the desires of my heart.
Please help me to live them.

Amen.

- THURSDAY 3 -
Dependence

Thank you, Lord, for the first meal of the day, which could consist of any number of good things—

orange juice, maybe, or grape or apple;
eggs, perhaps, or pancakes or bacon;
cereal, maybe, or oatmeal or muffins;
milk, perhaps, or coffee or tea.

Whatever we eat or drink this morning, it all comes from you; but

something produced it—the earth, the animal, the plant;
someone nurtured and harvested it—the farmers, in all their manifestations;
someone processed it, inspected it, packaged it, transported it, delivered it, priced it, sold it.

So as we sit down this morning and every morning to our breakfast, we will thank you. But in thanking you we will also thank everyone and everything you used to provide it for us.

O Lord, cause our gratitude for you and for others to multiply this morning and every morning so that it will last throughout this day and every day.

And free us from the illusion of independence and self-sufficiency by reminding us of how many people we depend on for our food and of how we ultimately depend on you.

Amen.

- THURSDAY 4 -
Partings

Today we will say "Hello," and we will say "Goodbye"—

"Hello" to people we are seeing for the first time today,
"Goodbye" to people we expect to see again tomorrow,

"Hello" to someone we are seeing for the very first time,
"Goodbye" to someone we are seeing for the very last time.

It is not morbidity but rather reality to face the fact that

we meet and we part,
we have and we have not,
we come and we go,
we live and we die.

Help us today, O Lord, to embrace the way of things so that we can embrace each other without clinging.

Help us to give each other over to you so that we can give ourselves to each other without fear.

Help us to be so fully present with each other that when the parting comes, the absence will be freighted not with the pain that accompanies an unexpected interruption but rather with the peace that follows an anticipated completion.

Amen.

- THURSDAY 5 -
The Edge

Today I will stand on the edge—but on the edge of what?

maybe the edge of chaos,
maybe the edge of despair,
maybe the edge of discouragement.

Or

maybe the edge of adventure,
maybe the edge of insight,
maybe the edge of grace.

O Lord, depending on which is right and best,
pull me back from the edge or push me over it.

Amen.

- THURSDAY 6 -
Presence

O Lord, we get drawn away from the moment by various distractions—fears, doubts, fantasies, and the like—all of which prevent us from being fully present.

Forgive our lack of gratitude for the moment in which we are. It is a great gift, and we repent of our failure to acknowledge it.

Give us greater single-mindedness so that we do not miss the blessings and opportunities in this moment.

Help us, Lord, to be fully present in each moment we live.

And never let us forget that you are present with us in each moment we live.

Amen.

- THURSDAY 7 -
Appearances

It is the way of things;
it is the way of us—

that we will think a lot about keeping the rules and about not breaking the laws;

that we will think a lot about appearances.

It is the way of things;
it is the way of us—

that we will think if we don't do any wrong anyone can see, then we're fine;

that if someone else does something wrong someone can see, then they're not fine—

and we will think a lot about appearances.

But God, today let it be the way of things;
let it be the way of us—

that we will know it is just possible that appearances are deceiving;

that just because we are seen doing what appears to be the right thing, it does not necessarily mean our hearts are in the right place;

that if someone else is seen doing what appears to be the wrong thing, it does not necessarily mean their heart is in the wrong place.

So tend to our hearts today, O Lord; help us to pay close attention to the state of our hearts—

guard us from self-righteousness and judgmentalism;
grant us self-awareness and grace.

Amen.

- THURSDAY 8 -
Determination

"Jesus set his face to go to Jerusalem," which means he was utterly determined to finish his course, to fulfill his calling, to do God's will, and to give himself up.

Where have we set our faces to go?
What are we determined to do?

Forgive us, Lord, when we set our faces to arrive at places to which following Jesus should not take us—places of ease, places of escape, places of self-satisfaction, places of security.

Forgive us, Lord, when we are determined to do things that do not befit the life of those who have taken up their cross and followed Jesus—to get our own way, to set our own agenda, to live for self first, to hoard stuff, to hoard blessings, to hoard forgiveness, to save our lives.

Where have we set our faces to go?
What are we determined to do?

Help us, Lord, to set our faces to arrive at places to which following Jesus should take us—places of service, places of sacrifice, places of mystery, places of risk, places of wonder, places of openness, places of vulnerability, places of grace.

Help us, Lord, to be determined to do things that befit the life of those who have taken up their cross and followed Jesus—

to do things in your way;
to follow your agenda;
to live for you first, others second, and self last;
to share our stuff;
to share our blessings;
to share our forgiveness;
to sacrifice our lives.

Grant, O Lord, that we will set our faces to go to our Jerusalem, so that we will be utterly determined to finish our course, to fulfill our calling, to do your will, and to give ourselves up.

Amen.

- THURSDAY 9 -
Practice

"Be ye perfect," the Book says, "as your Father in heaven is perfect."

"Practice makes perfect," the saying has it.

So Lord, today help us to practice—

to practice radical grace,
to practice radical love,
to practice radical trust,
to practice radical forgiveness,
to practice radical faithfulness—

so that we will move farther along toward the kind of maturity, completeness, and integrity that befit the children of God.

And help us to live with and in and through the knowledge that we will need to practice every day from now on and for as long as we live—which means we will never quite make it—until, by your grace, we open our eyes and find that we have.

Amen.

- THURSDAY 10 -
Slow and Steady

Slow and steady may or may not win the race, but it sure will help keep you from losing your mind—and your way.

So slow me down, Lord; help me to take time really

to see what is around me,
to be with the person in front of me,
to pay attention to the meaning of things happening around me,
to consider what you have to do with it all.

So steady me, Lord; help me to lean on you so that

my eyes can stay on the goal toward which you are moving me,
my pride and illusion of independence can be supplanted by humility and trust,
my heart can become more and more focused on loving you and loving others,
my life can become grounded in the things that last and do not pass away.

Slow me down, Lord, and steady me.

Amen.

- THURSDAY 11 -
One

The church, the body of Christ, is one body.

Forgive us, Lord, for the ways in which we deny our oneness, in which we deny the unity that is your legacy in us.

Remind us that it takes all of the members of the body, each faithfully carrying out its function, for the body to be healthy.

Help us, Lord, to celebrate the differences and the diversity that are basic to our oneness in you.

Help us to live out the truth that, because we are your one body, we are vitally connected to, indeed, belong to you—and to each other.

Amen.

- THURSDAY 12 -
Persecution

Do I have any enemies? I think I can honestly say there is no one of whom I think as an enemy. Is there someone who thinks of me as an enemy? I hope not. But there probably is.

If there are, I hope they are wrong; I hope they regard me in wrong ways and for wrong reasons.

But if their reasons for so regarding me are justified and rational and based in fact, I hope they will forgive me. I pray, oh Lord, that you will forgive me.

Regardless, I do not feel persecuted; I do not feel like anyone is out to get me. If anyone is, unbeknownst to me, I ask you, Lord, to bless them and not to curse them, even as I also ask you to change them. And if it is I who needs to change, change me.

Forgive us, Lord, when we call persecution what is not persecution—
small slights or mild criticisms or even cruel remarks or unfounded attacks.
Lord, in our context they do not rise to the level of what followers of yours in other contexts are really experiencing—

who are being economically marginalized,
whose basic human rights are being curtailed,
who are being imprisoned,
who are being executed—

and to claim that we as Western Christians are being persecuted is an insult to those in other places who really are.

Lord, would you ask them to bless and not to curse those who persecute them?

I suppose you would.

In that case,

Lord, have mercy.
Christ, have mercy.

And inspire the rest of us to work toward a world in which they won't have reason anymore to pray that prayer.

Amen.

- THURSDAY 13 -
Artistry

The day in front of me is like a canvas awaiting the artist's touch.

It is not blank; all the work done to this point in preparation for this day's efforts is already on it.

Yet it is not a paint-by-numbers scene; choices and decisions have to be made—and they matter.

Moreover, there is more than one artist.

I am one artist.

All the other people in my life, be they central or peripheral, are artists, too.

Then there is you—The Artist.

Sometimes the painting gets messy, what with all those hands involved in the work.

But sometimes I get a glimpse of a great order showing itself.

Help me, O Lord, to be faithful in my efforts to paint my part as best I can.
Help all of us to be faithful in our efforts to paint our parts as best we can.

And help us to have great trust in the fact that you, The Great Artist, are guiding the entire endeavor.

We trust in and praise you and look toward the emerging masterpiece.

Amen.

- THURSDAY 14 (OR MAUNDY THURSDAY) -
Like Jesus

Jesus, the Son of God, the Messiah,

healed people,
served people, and
gave his life for people.

What are we who follow him doing to

heal people,
serve people, and
give our lives for people?

O God, may Jesus become so alive in us that we cannot help but live his way today and every day.

Amen.

- THURSDAY 15 -
Crises

A crisis is an event after which things will never be the same.

The first one of the day has already come, been lived through, and gone—
I got out of bed.

Most crises are small and pass without my noticing—the shifts and turns and choices that are almost imperceptible but that still make a big difference.

Thank you for the grace of such unawareness; it keeps me more or less sane.

But then there are the big ones—the problems, the conflicts, the eruptions, the situations—that, when they crop up and as they are lived through, I and everyone else involved in them know that something important, and if not earth-shaking at least us-shaking, is going on.

Thank you, Lord, for the crises, whether small or large, because change is part of life and is to be embraced and lived into.

O God, fill me with trust and courage and grace so that I might not fear the crises and the accompanying changes, but rather live through them with my eyes on how things will be on the other side even though I can't quite see over that horizon.

My daily crises are, after all, good practice for the last big crisis, for the final change, that will inevitably come.

Amen.

- THURSDAY 16 -
Praying Well

O Lord,

As we pray, please change our hearts so that our praying is transformed.

Our tendency is to pray for what we need; we confess that our prayers can be self-ish and can spring from motives of self-protection and self-preservation and even self-promotion.

The Lord Jesus taught us through his words, through his life, and through his death that the most meaningful life is

the risked life rather than the protected life,
the sacrificed life rather than the preserved life,
the given life rather than the kept life,
the shared life rather than the hoarded life,
the emptied life rather than the filled life.

We need to live such lives, but we need help to live them—and we need to ask for your help if we are going to live them.

Teach us to ask for help to live as you are calling us as followers of Jesus Christ to live.

Amen.

- THURSDAY 17 -
Was

Thank you, Lord, for what was.

Everything that has happened in our lives up to this point has served to make us who we are.

Some of it has been good and positive and constructive and helpful, while some of it has been bad and negative and destructive and hurtful, and some of it has been just so-so.

But all of it has been real; all of it has been ours; all of it has been life.

There were times that could have been better had we been better, but we weren't and so they weren't and there's no point stewing over that.

Besides, there were times that could have been worse had we been worse, but we weren't and so they weren't.

Help us, Lord, to learn our lessons from what was.
Help us not to live in what was.
Help us to be grateful for what was.
Help us to see how you were there in what was.

Amen.

- THURSDAY 18 -
Reflexes

There are things we do reflexively, without thinking, that are absolutely vital to our living—breathing, for example, or swallowing or blinking. Such reflexive actions are natural to us.

Our goal is to have some other actions become natural and reflexive to us because they are just as vital to our living—trusting, for example, or loving or forgiving.

Those behaviors, though, are not innate; they must be acquired, or perhaps better put, they must be received—from you, only from you.

Give us, Lord, the grace we need to receive them.

Having been received by and through your grace, such behaviors must then be nurtured and developed and practiced if they are going to move toward being natural and reflexive to us. They are gifts that must be worked on and with if they are going to become natural to us; it is an irony, but it is the truth.

Give us, Lord, the discipline we need to develop them.

Perhaps we must accept that trusting and loving and forgiving will never become as reflexive to us as are breathing and swallowing and blinking.

But by your grace and by our discipline they can get mighty close—much closer than we think. May our acceptance of that truth become more and more natural and reflexive to us, too.

Amen.

- THURSDAY 19 -
Striving

We admit, O God, if we strived for more, we would have more; that we don't achieve the maturity in faith and hope and love that is possible because we don't put in the effort.

Forgive us for our sometimes lack of striving.

But we affirm, O God, that the best things of all come to us without our striving for them; they are gifts of your grace—your love, for example, and the salvation that is ours in Christ Jesus our Lord.

Forgive us for our tendency to strive for what we can't reach through our own efforts but must be simply and gratefully received and accepted.

Help us to accept gratefully what is ours in you.
Help us to strive to develop what is ours in you.

Amen.

- THURSDAY 20 -
Simplicity

We have so many things to do.
We have so many things on our minds.
We have so many people saying so many things.
We have so many problems within us and around us.

It's no wonder it all can feel so very, very complicated.

Lord, please give us simplicity in our lives.

In praying that prayer, we aren't asking for the realities of life to go away and we aren't asking to be exempt from the struggles that come with being human.

We are asking, though,
for singleness of mind,
for singleness of heart,
for singleness of focus.

May our lives be focused on the one thing of loving and serving you, for in that is found true simplicity.

Amen.

- THURSDAY 21 -
When

"When" is a powerful word because it points us toward the future.

In pointing us toward the future, "when" can give us hope.

If we say "when" and then follow it with some dream or goal and then set about (a) doing what we can to fulfill the dream or arrive at the goal and (b) trusting God to take care of the big picture—of the details we can't envision or the obstacles we can't overcome—then "when" is a positive force.

But in pointing us toward the future, "when" can also give us excuses.

If we say "when" and then follow it with some dream or goal and then set about (a) doing little or nothing to bring it about and (b) failing to cultivate trust in God to work things out that we can't work out, then "when" is a negative force.

O God, help us when we say "when" to be filled with hope for the future that we in your grace have. Cause that hope to be an active hope so that we might do all in our power to make happen what needs to happen. Cause that hope to be a trusting hope so that we might trust you to see and know and do what only you can see and know and do.

Give us a healthy balance, dear God, between living in peace with the way things are and living in hope for the way things need to be.

Amen.

- THURSDAY 22 -

Courage

There are times when it is hard to know what is the right position to take or the right stand to make. Sometimes both sides have their points.

There are also times when the lines between right and wrong are clear. Sometimes our side is chosen for us if we are true to the Light that has been given to us.

There are also those rare times when in our place and context to choose what seems right to us means we might have to stand alone. Sometimes being true to ourselves and being true to our following of our Lord means standing there with no one at our side except him.

Lord, we don't ask for attention, admiration, or martyrdom; we just ask for the ability to have integrity in our hearts under you and then to live out of that integrity.

Show us where to stand.
Give us courage to stand there.

And please—whether we stand alone or with a few or with many—
stand there with us.

Amen.

- THURSDAY 23 -

Incentives

We are urged on by incentives—the raise, the promotion, the honor, the thanks, the prestige, and so on, which is understandable. Ambition in and of itself is not a bad thing.

But Lord, if we are going to be whole and sound, we need better and higher incentives than those.

Cause us to be urged on by a desire to walk with you, to serve others, to do good.

May your love and grace, working in us and through us, be our ultimate incentives. Such love and grace are, in the final analysis, their own reward.

Amen.

- THURSDAY 24 -
Ordinary

Is anything really "ordinary"?

We use the word to mean "run of the mill," "not unusual," "regular," and "expected."

But should we regard anything in those ways?

After all, everything is a gift and all of life is grace. And it is in the ordinary that the most extraordinary things happen and the most extraordinary truths are discovered and the most extraordinary relationships are developed.

Help us, O God, to regard no moment, no day, no experience, no conversation, no person, no breath, as ordinary.

May we rather be filled with a sense of the wonder of it all.

Amen.

- THURSDAY 25 -
Up

Keep us looking up, Lord—

up toward you,
up toward where we are headed,
up toward what we are becoming—

for it is in looking up that we are inspired.

But at the same time,

Keep us looking down, Lord—

down at where you have placed us,
down at who you have placed us with,
down at what we need to be right here and right now—

for it is in looking down that we are grounded.

Keep us looking up and keep us looking down so that our inspiration will feed our groundedness and our groundedness will feed our inspiration.

Amen.

- THURSDAY 26 -
Hospitality

For your hospitality—for the way in which you welcome us into your home, into your family, and into your life—we thank you, God.

For the hospitality of others—for the way in which friends and neighbors and sometimes even strangers welcome us into their home, into their family, and into their life—we thank you, God.

For the hospitality your love and grace in us compel us to show to friends and neighbors and sometimes even strangers, we thank you, God.

And since we can never be too hospitable or welcoming, increase our love, increase our grace, and increase our desire and willingness to be hospitable.

Amen.

- THURSDAY 27 -
Consciousness

It is one of the things—maybe the main thing—that makes us human, this consciousness we have, this self-awareness, this sense of self.

In it lies our potential for a sense of purpose, a sense of calling, a sense of power —and a sense of you.

But in it also lies our potential for a sense of angst, a sense of meaninglessness, a sense of impotence, and a sense of your absence.

It makes a difference which potential we feed and nourish and develop.

Yet there are dangers down either path.

It is better to develop the positive potential in our consciousness, but in doing so we need to guard against putting self first and against thinking it is all about us.

If we spend too much energy and time developing the negative potential in our consciousness—while we need to be aware of and accepting of that side of ourselves—we will find ourselves beset by anxiety and fear and even hopelessness.

Help us, O God, to accept our possibilities and our limitations, to live in hope and in reality, and to dwell in the light of self-understanding and with a healthy curiosity about what we don't yet know about ourselves.

Thank you for our awareness of your presence. When we doubt it, remind us —whatever it takes.

Amen.

- THURSDAY 28 -
Thanks

To say "Thank you" when someone gives you something is to be polite.
To really mean it from the bottom of your heart is to be grateful.

We thank you, O God, for everything, because without you nothing is and so apart from you nothing comes to us.

Cause us to be so grateful to you that we live in a constant state of thanksgiving, thereby avoiding the error of attributing our blessings to ourselves or to someone or something else and rather cultivating an awareness of our dependence and your grace.

We give you thanks, O God—from the bottom of our hearts.

Amen.

- THURSDAY 29 -
Rhythm

A life, like a song, needs a rhythm; it needs a steady flow that comes to feel familiar and appropriate and right.

But sometimes in life, like in a song, the rhythm gets broken; an unexpected shift, a surprising note, or a jarring change of key occurs.

It can be surprising and even disconcerting; we may not like it at first.

But then we come to realize it is the shift or the change that makes it—the song or the life—interesting.

Thank you, God, for the rhythm of our lives, for the usual and the expected.

Thank you also, though, for the shifts in rhythm and for the changes in key that make us sit up and pay closer attention.

Help us to embrace it all as part of our song—as part of our life.

Amen.

- THURSDAY 30 -
Convergence

Every day in many places and for many reasons a number of people—sometimes a small number, sometimes a large number, sometimes a middling one—will converge on a particular place for a particular purpose.

Sometimes the purpose is deliberately chosen;
sometimes it is arrived at randomly or accidentally.

Sometimes the purpose is a positive and productive one;
sometimes it is a negative and destructive one.

Sometimes the convergence is a reunion of old friends;
sometimes it is a gathering of strangers.

The bottom line in such convergences is commonality of purpose.

Guide our steps, O Lord—guide our thoughts and our motives and our choice of compatriots—so that when we converge with others upon a place for a purpose we will leave it and the world better for our having been in on it together.

Help us to keep our eyes and hearts focused on that great eternal convergence that you in your grace and sovereignty—the fulfilling of your ultimate purpose—are working out.

And cause us to live out here and now the prelude to that great convergence that exists when those who realize your grace come together to serve you.

Amen.

- THURSDAY 31 -
Matter

Over the last few days I spent time with hundreds of people I will probably never see again, with some people I may come across again down the road, with a few people I have known for a long time and almost surely will encounter again in the future, and with at least one person who knows me better than anyone and with whom I would gladly spend every waking moment were it possible.

Some of those people are naturally more important to me than are others, but each of them—I hope every one of them—is vitally important to at least one other person.

Before long there will be, the experts say, more than seven billion people living on this planet.

I wish I could honestly say they all matter to me, but what would such an assertion mean anyway?

But I believe what your Book says when it affirms that you made and care for every last one of them—that they all matter to you enough that your Son died for them.

O God, help them all to know that they matter. O God, help me to treat those who matter to me in ways that will make it clear to them.

O God, help my heart and spirit and life to grow so that I will have room for more people to matter to me.

Amen.

- THURSDAY 32 -
Useful

Things need to be done.
People need to be helped.

There are things we can do.
There are ways we can help.

Help us, Lord, to be useful today. Help us to do that which we can do and to help those whom we can help.

Give us insight to know the most constructive ways to be helpful; give us grace to help in ways that will share the love and grace of our Lord Jesus Christ.

Then, we will be useful in the Kingdom of God, which is the most valuable usefulness of all.

Amen.

- THURSDAY 33 -
Think

These brains of ours are magnificent things; thank you, God, for giving them to us.

The experts say we make use of very little of the brain that's available to us; forgive us, God, for not taking full advantage of our intellectual capacity.

O Lord, help us to think about

what we say before we say it,
what we do before we do it, and
where we go before we go there.

O Lord, help us to think on

the things that will help us to grow in our relationship with you,
the things that will help us to grow in our relationship with others, and
the things that will help us to grow into the likeness of Christ our Lord.

O Lord, help us to think on

clearly,
soberly, and
reverently.

O Lord, help us not to think

things that are not productive,
things that are not helpful, and
things that are not of you.

And Lord, help us not to think so much about

how we need to change that we don't change,
how we need to act that we don't get around to acting, and
how we need to love that we don't get around to loving.

Amen.

- THURSDAY 34 -
Pleasure

Thank you, God, for the ability to feel pleasure and for the blessing, when it comes, of feeling it.

We can feel pleasure through touch, through sight, through sound, through smell, through taste. Thank you for the physical pleasures of life.

Thank you for those sensations when they come to us. Help us, though, not to seek them as if life is to be built around them and as if the painful experiences of life are less valuable than the pleasurable ones.

We can also feel pleasure in our spirits; it comes when we have a moment or an extended period of gratitude for our blessings or of peace because we sense we are in a good place in our relationship with you.

Thank you for those sensations when they come to us. Help us, though, not to seek them in a way that causes us to try to escape the painful spiritual experiences of life as if they are less meaningful and helpful than the pleasurable ones.

Thank you for pleasure, O Lord.

Help us to enjoy it but not to live for it.

Amen.

- THURSDAY 35 -
Reciprocity

Today I can do unto others as they do unto me; I can base my treatment of them on their treatment of me.

Or I can do unto others as I think they deserve; I can evaluate their character and worthiness and act toward them according to my evaluation of them.

In either case I am reciprocating according to what they do to me or according to who they are or seem to me to be. My track record shows I will sometimes reciprocate in those ways. Lord, forgive me.

Help me instead to do as Jesus said:
"Do unto others as you would have them do unto you."

Help me to reciprocate not according to how they treat me or how they seem to me, but instead according to how I would want them to be toward me.

But Lord, there is some danger even here.

What do I want them to do to me?
How do I want them to treat me?
How do I feel about myself?

If I think too highly of myself, I might want them to coddle me and to flatter me; it would do me no good to be treated like that, and it would do them no good for me to treat them like that.

If I think too little of myself, I might want them to punish me or to persecute me; it would do me no good to be treated like that, and it would do them no good for me to treat them like that.

So Lord, please give me a good, clear, and honest view of who I am; give me a realistic view of myself that includes the difference your love and grace make in me.

Then cause me, in light of that clear view and honest vision of who I am, to see others like I want to be seen and to treat them like I want to be treated.

Amen.

- THURSDAY 36 -
Before

On the one hand, what happened before is over and done with; on the other hand, what happened before is still with us and is a part of us.

Help us, Lord, not to let what happened before be a source of paralyzing guilt or mesmerizing nostalgia or interfering regret.

Help us also, Lord, to let what happened before be a source of enlightening education and edifying correction and personal formation.

Even as we acknowledge and celebrate the truth that we are the product of everything that has gone on before in our lives, empower us not to be victims of what has gone on before in our lives.

We thank you, Lord, for what has happened before.

We repent, Lord, of what has happened before.

We move on, Lord, in the light of what has happened before
—but not in its shadow.

Amen.

- THURSDAY 37 -
Just

"I'm just a regular guy."
"I'm just a farmer."
"I'm just a homemaker."
"I'm just a preacher."
"I'm just a layperson."
"I'm just a wife and mother."
"I'm just a husband and father."
"I'm just a nurse."
"I'm just a businessperson."
"I'm just a __________."

We can all fill in the blank because we all say things like that because we all are things like that.

O God, give us grace to live in the power and wonder of "just" because it is exactly in the ordinariness and the routine and the anonymity of our lives that almost all of our living is done and most of our meaning is found.

Our ordinariness is the realm within which we know and show almost all of the love and grace and mercy and forgiveness and sacrifice we will know and show.

"I'm just me."

Thanks be to God.

Amen.

- THURSDAY 38 -
Exclamation Point

An exclamation point is the only mark of punctuation that clearly communicates emotion. When you see one at the end of a sentence you know right away that, had you heard the person speak that sentence, it would have been with surprise or delight or amazement or excitement or pain or panic or the like.

Exclamation points aren't typically used as much in writing or in speaking as are periods or question marks because normal everyday living and the descriptions or accounts of it involve more statements and questions than exclamations or interjections.

Exclamation points mark the emphatic or surprising or unusual or shocking moments of life—the ones that stop us in our tracks.

O God, we thank you for the routine of life, for the fact that typically life involves more statements and questions than exclamations and interjections.

At the same time, we thank you for the moments and the events that prompt an "Aha!" or even an "Oh no!" because they remind and teach us that life is not predictable, that it is not under our control, that it can and does surprise us.

Help us, O God, not to live in search of or in need of exclamation points in life.

Help us rather to live in readiness for and in expectation of them.

They are not what life is all about. But when they come, they are briefly—but powerfully—all we can see or feel because in those moments everything else seems to go away. Perhaps, then, they are practice for what will happen when we see you face to face!

Amen.

- THURSDAY 39 -
Images

Images are substitutes for the real thing.

The impulse to create or to adopt them and to give our allegiance to them is understandable because when it comes to God, the real thing is hard to grasp.

But that's the point: God is God and as God, God cannot be grasped. God cannot be held onto or held down. God cannot be maneuvered and manipulated. God cannot be controlled.

Forgive us, Lord, when we try. Forgive us for the ways we will substitute a church or a theological position or a project or a mission or a program or a leader or a political movement or a cause for you. Forgive us for the ways we will give ourselves over to such things either because we have some control over them or because we find it easy to let them have control over us.

Give us the faith and the courage, O God, to worship you in spirit and in truth and to walk with you in all your mystery and wonder and freedom.

We praise you and thank you for the images of yourself you sanction.

First, we thank you that we, your human creation, are made in your image. Give us grace and strength to bear your image in the world and not to shirk our responsibility by looking to something or someone outside ourselves to be for us and to do for us what it is our calling to be and to do.

Second, we thank you that you sent your Son Jesus into the world as your absolute image so that we might be able to understand both you and ourselves better.

Help us, O God, to model the way we live out being your image in the world on the way in which our Lord Jesus Christ lived out being your image in the world.

Amen.

- THURSDAY 40 -
Respect

She is her, and I am me.
His is his, and mine is mine.
We are us, and ours is ours.

Help us, Lord, to remember those basic rules of life so that we will treat each other and ourselves with the respect we are as individuals and as a community due.

Cause us not to misuse or abuse or manipulate another person or group of people for the sake of our personal or economic gratification or advantage; cause us rather to want and to work for the independence, health, and fulfillment of the other.

Cause us not to build up what we have on the backs of others without allowing them their due nor to participate in structures and systems that foster such a practice; cause us rather to work alongside and with others for our mutual good and benefit and for society's good and benefit.

Cause us not to value our things and our stuff too highly nor to value someone else's things and stuff too highly; cause us rather to develop a healthy gratitude for just having enough and a healthy thankfulness for the ways another is blessed.

Cause us to be much less motivated by having and taking; cause us to be much more motivated by giving and sharing.

Amen.

- THURSDAY 41 -
Touch

A touch is inappropriate when it is unwanted or uninvited or unwelcomed or hurtful or manipulative or abusive.

A touch is appropriate when it is wanted or invited or welcomed or helpful or selfless or healing.

Thank you, God, for the touches offered to us by those who love us and who care about us and who want to comfort or encourage or strengthen us; help us to accept such touches as the gift they are.

Thank you, God, for the chance to offer touches to others because we love them and care about them and want to comfort or encourage or strengthen them; help us to offer such touches as the gift they are.

Bless those, O God, whose lives are for whatever reason—and there can be many, both self-inflicted and other-inflicted—bereft of the touch that helps and heals. Give them the gift of such a touch, and make us open to being the hand through which you touch them with your grace and love.

Amen.

- THURSDAY 42 -

Dust

We are dust, and to dust we shall return. So says your Book, and so says our experience.

It is easy, though, when we live in a society that landscapes or paves over so much of its dust, to lose our connection with the dust from which we came and to which we shall return.

Perhaps those societies that walk in and live with the dust keep more of a connection with it; perhaps it would behoove the rest of us to work in the dirt of a garden or to walk barefoot in the dirt on some regular basis so that we may stay in touch with our physical roots.

Give us grace, O Lord, always to remember that we are dust.

At the same time, give us grace always to remember that you made the dust and so you made us.

Give us grace also to remember that you in your love sent your Son to be formed from the same dust as we are—and that has made all the difference in this dustiness of ours.

Amen.

- THURSDAY 43 -

Lost

To be lost means either (a) you don't know where you are or (b) you know where you are but don't know how to get from there to where you need to be.

We've all been lost and we all get lost; we all know the great sense of relief that comes from being found.

Lostness while it lasts is made bearable by the knowledge that someone loves you enough to look for you.

Thank you, O God, that when we are lost you look for us.

Thank you, O God, that we know the joy that comes from being found.

Thank you, O God, that if we are lost or get lost today we know you will be looking for us.

Cause us, O God, to prefer being found to being lost, to prefer a sense of your presence to a sense of your absence, and to prefer the peace of dwelling in you to the freedom of wandering away from you.

Amen.

- THURSDAY 44 -
Sigh

Sometimes we sigh as an expression of contentment.

Hear our sighs, O Lord, and accept the grateful thanksgiving they express.

Sometimes we sigh as an expression of exasperation.

Hear our sighs, O Lord, and accept the plea for patience they express.

Sometimes we sigh as an expression of fatigue.

Hear our sighs, O Lord, and accept the yearning for rest they express.

Our sighs express feelings and thoughts and awareness that go beneath and beyond words; they express what we feel and think and know at the very core of our beings.

Our sighs, in other words, express our deepest and most heartfelt prayers.

Thank you, O God, for hearing and accepting and understanding them.

Amen.

- THURSDAY 45 -

Me

Try as I might to make it be otherwise, all of my experience starts with me. "Me" is my default setting; "me" is my perspective; "me" is my vantage point.

I would very much like to be able to see things first from the point of view of other people; I would like to be able to be so attuned to the situation and plight of others that I consider how events affect them before I consider how they affect me.

I would even more like to be able to see things first from your point of view, O God; I would like to be able to be so immersed in my relationship with you and so intimate in my fellowship with your Spirit that I see as you see and evaluate as you evaluate and discern as you discern.

I know, though, that I will have to receive and to be glad for any bit of progress I can make in those areas for, no matter how much I can grow in seeing things as others see them and as you see them, I will always be me.

So God, please do your gracious work in me. Mold me and make me; form me and shape me. Help me to grow every day toward being the most complete and mature version of me I can become.

For it is in such wholeness that I can best grow in my empathy with others and in my identification with you.

So thank you, Lord, for me.
And help me, Lord, to become me.

Amen.

- THURSDAY 46 -

Consent

Consent is assent that takes a little more convincing.

Consent tends, then, to be given in response to pressure; someone has a point of view or a proposed course of action in which they want us to join, and they set about selling it to us. To buy into it is to consent.

Sometimes consent is given because

we are convinced of the rightness of an idea;
we are too weak to oppose what we believe to be a flawed idea;
we are too lazy to think for ourselves;
we feel pressure from someone who seems to control our happiness or future;
we'd rather get along than not, even if getting along means violating our principles.

Lord, give us proper perspective on the pressure that is brought to bear on us to think or to act in certain ways. Form in us a spirit that wants to be open to better ways of thinking and acting, but that filters proposals through the kind of grace and love seen in Jesus Christ and communicated through the Holy Spirit.

Lord, constantly remind us that our lives ultimately are in your hands and not in the hands of any person, regardless of that person's authority over us. Remind us that we should consent to someone else's idea only if we can honestly see such consent as consent to you.

May our giving in to someone never be a giving up to them; but may our giving in to someone always be a giving up to you.

Amen.

- THURSDAY 47 -
Praise

Praise be to God for our lives; help us to praise you for them, O God, by living them to their fullest.

Praise be to God for the food, water, shelter, and clothing we have; help us to praise you for those essentials, O God, by doing all we can to help those who lack them.

Praise be to God for the good earth on which we live; help us to praise you for it, O God, by loving and protecting our home planet.

Praise be to God for our families; help us to praise you for them, O God, by working more for the good and happiness of our family members than for our own.

Praise be to God for Jesus Christ our Lord; help us to praise you for him, O God, by following Jesus in the ways of love, grace, service, and sacrifice.

Praise be to God for the ability to praise God; help us to praise you for that ability, O God, by remembering every day to exercise it.

Amen.

- THURSDAY 48 -
Depend

We say, "You can depend on me," by which we mean to say that someone can be assured that when needed we will be there. No matter what the circumstances are, we are saying, we will be right there beside the one who needs us.

We also say, "It all depends," by which we mean to say that our particular response to a situation is contingent on the way events play out and on the way circumstances develop. We will be there, we are saying, but the manner in which we will be there must be left flexible until the actual need can be clarified.

O God, form us into dependable people who pay attention to what is really happening so that our dependability will translate into genuine helpfulness.

Remind us, O God, of your dependability. We praise you for the fact you are always there for us. Cause us to realize that the particular way you are there for us in a particular instance depends on our circumstances and our choices and our context and any number of factors, some of which we are aware and many of which we are not.

We can depend on you to be there for us.

What that means—whether it means you will be there to comfort or to afflict, to confirm or to correct, to convince or to convict, to pick up or to push down, to heal or to hurt—well, that all depends.

Help us to trust that the way you exhibit your dependability is always in the way appropriate to the situation.

Amen.

- THURSDAY 49 -
Contrariness

On the one hand, O God, forgive us for and take away from us our contrariness, that state of mind and stance toward life that makes us

disagreeable rather than helpful,
negative rather than realistic,
pessimistic rather than optimistic,
argumentative rather than deliberative,
uncooperative rather than cooperative.

On the other hand, O God, confirm in us and fill us even more with your contrariness, that state of mind and stance toward life that makes us

loving rather than unloving,
forgiving rather than unforgiving,
broad-minded rather than small-minded,
open rather than closed,
hopeful rather than hopeless,
generous rather than selfish.

There is a contrariness that comes from us and helps no one, including us; cause it to decrease in us.

There is a contrariness that comes from you and helps everyone, including us; cause it to increase in us.

Amen.

- THURSDAY 50 -
Sensitive

On the one hand, we can be too sensitive, too attuned to what everyone else thinks about us or says about us—or to what we think they think or say about us.

Lord, protect us from the self-centeredness that lives and listens as if everything is all about us and that looks to find reasons to be lifted up or to be put down.

On the other hand, we can be not sensitive enough; we can be too unattuned to what is going on in the world around us, to the people around us, and to the spirit within us.

Lord, grow in us a spirit that with grace and maturity deals with the effects life has on us, but that is more attuned to the needs and hurts and joys of others than it is to those of self.

On the one hand, make us less sensitive.
On the other hand, make us more sensitive.

Amen.

- THURSDAY 51 -
Dangers

Protect us, O God, from the dangers that lurk this time of year.

Protect us from the danger of wanting too much from the season.
Protect us from the danger of expecting too little from the season.

Protect us from the danger of giving too much of ourselves to others.
Protect us from the danger of giving too little of ourselves to others.

Protect us from the danger of demanding that our culture pay more attention to Jesus.
Protect us from the danger of not demanding that our churches pay more attention to Jesus.

Protect us from the danger of neglecting the poor and hurting at Christmas.
Protect us from the danger of neglecting the poor and hurting before and after Christmas.

Protect us from the danger of excess and wantonness.
Protect us from the danger of mirthlessness and joylessness.

Protect us, O God, from the dangers that lurk this time of year.

Amen.

- THURSDAY 52 -

Sinner

Because I am human,
I am a sinner.

Because I am proud,
I am a sinner.

Because I am foolish,
I am a sinner.

Because I am afraid,
I am a sinner.

Because I am stubborn,
I am a sinner.

Because I am me,
I am a sinner.

Because I am a sinner—and because you are a gracious God—
I am forgiven.

I acknowledge my state, O God. But even more, I celebrate your grace and the difference your grace makes in my state.

Amen.

Friday Prayers

- FRIDAY 1 -

Choices

Hundreds of choices I will make today, O Lord.

Some I will make after much thought;
others I will make without a thought.

Some will seem large;
others will seem small.

Some will appear significant;
others will appear insignificant.

But they will all matter, because in each case I could choose another way—maybe even many other ways—and another way chosen could lead to a different outcome.

I do not ask that I always make the right choice or the best choice, for experience and history and honesty tell me I will not, I cannot.

I only ask that, by your Spirit within me, my motivations—the forces that drive my choices—be the same as those that drove those of the Lord Jesus, that I be compelled by grace and love and mercy and obedience to choose what I choose this day.

Amen.

- FRIDAY 2 -

Responsibilities

Responsibilities are my constant companions, O God, and I will carry them today as I do every day.

I thank you for them; for to be an adult is to be responsible, and one goal of life is to be grown up about it all.

But I need your help because sometimes, even when the responsibilities I have are ones I want, and especially when they are ones I don't, they get heavy; sometimes they feel a lot like burdens.

I don't ask that they be taken away;
I would not abdicate my hard-earned adulthood.

I do ask that they not be complicated by faulty motives, by self-centered scheming, by anxious fretting, and especially by a failure to keep love for you and for others as my ultimate aim in living and in carrying out my responsibilities.

In other words, Lord, help me not to make it all about me, because it is in losing my life that I will find it.

Amen.

- FRIDAY 3 -
Perspective

Give me perspective, O Lord, perspective to know

that I am not the center of the universe;
that this is not all there is;
that without you I am not.

Give me perspective, O Lord, perspective to know

that I am your cherished and beloved child;
that each day on earth is a unique opportunity;
that with you I am.

Give me perspective, O Lord, perspective to know

the truth about me,
the truth about you,
the truth that will set me free.

Amen.

- FRIDAY 4 -

Unbidden

O God,

your grace covers me,
your love enfolds me,
your mercy blankets me

unbidden,
undeserved.

Today make me a channel for

your grace,
your love,
your mercy.

May the people I encounter be touched when

your grace,
your love,
your mercy

come from you,
through me,
to them

unbidden,
undeserved.

Amen.

- FRIDAY 5 -
Stretching

It's all a stretch, O Lord—

to exhibit grace,
to offer forgiveness,
to practice love,
to embrace suffering,
to follow Jesus,
to expect resurrection,
to anticipate heaven—

a stretch to trust in you.

So stretch me, Lord, tug and yank me—

inward toward the self you are pulling me to be,
outward toward the others you are pulling me to love,
upward toward the you whom you are pulling me to know,
toward the person you are pulling me to become,
toward the heaven you are pulling me to reach—

stretch me to trust in you.

I confess, O Lord, that my willingness to stretch, to respond to your tugs and yanks, will likely continue to be inconsistent, but I thank you that with each stretch I inch closer to the goal. And I pray that, after those times when the tension created by the stretch causes me to snap back toward where and who I was before, I will find, when the next stretch comes, I have at least become more flexible.

Amen.

- FRIDAY 6 -
Struggles

People we know and love are struggling, Lord, struggling with

sickness,
injury,
sadness,
disillusionment,
disappointment,
worry,
purpose,
direction,
understanding.

They may be struggling with others or with themselves or, whether they know it or not, they may be struggling with you—or with others, themselves, and you all at the same time.

Help them to know, O Lord, that not every struggle with is a struggle against, that some struggles are necessary and beneficial and even good.

Help them to know also, Lord, that you are struggling beside them, that you are struggling on their behalf and for their benefit—even if, odd as it may seem, their struggle is in some with way with you.

Help us as their friends and loved ones to struggle beside them, on their behalf and for their benefit—even if, odd as it may seem, their struggle is in some way with us.

And please help us in our struggles, too.

Amen.

- FRIDAY 7 -
Tests

We will be tested today, and the tests will come in many forms to some of which we are accustomed and for some of which we can prepare. We know that we can expect to be tested when we must choose between

putting you first and putting you anywhere else,
practicing forgiveness and seeking vengeance,
talking with someone and talking about someone,
worshiping you and worshiping stuff,
developing faith and living in fear,
speaking the truth in love and speaking the truth with malice,
being selfless and being selfish, and
following Jesus and following anyone else.

Help us, Lord, to go into this day with our eyes, minds, and spirits wide open, ready with your help to pass the tests we know are coming.

As for the tests that will come out of nowhere, unexpected and unanticipated and at this moment unimaginable and unfathomable, Lord, have mercy.

Amen.

- FRIDAY 8 -
Whelmed

To be whelmed, the dictionary says, is to be overcome. Events can whelm us. So can people.

Help us, Lord, not to be overwhelmed, to be whelmed too much, by events, that can too easily happen—given all the big and bad things that go on in the world, given our simultaneously helpful and unhelpful technological ability to know about most of it right away, and given our tendency to be involved in too many things at one time, some of which are important and some of which are not, but all of which take up our time and energy and attention.

Help us, Lord, not to be overwhelmed by people, which can too easily happen—given the legitimate needs all people have as well as the unfortunate and unnecessary chronic neediness so many people live out in the ways they think and behave, both of which can drain our emotional and spiritual resources whether necessarily or unnecessarily.

Protect us, O Lord, from caring too much.

But also help us, Lord, not to be underwhelmed, to be whelmed not enough, by events because things that happen nearby and far away, to us and to others, for good and bad, do matter and what we do when we can and as we can does make a difference.

Help us, Lord, not to be underwhelmed by people, not to become dulled and even immune to their needs—and even their presence—out of exasperation or self-preservation for, as understandable as that is, it is hard to see how we can be Christian and not give of ourselves for the sake of others.

Protect us, O Lord, from caring too little.

Give us balance, O Lord, that we be neither overwhelmed nor underwhelmed.

Give us faith, O Lord, so that we will know finally it is up to you and not up to us.

Give us grace, O Lord, so that we will share it however we can in every situation and with every person who needs it.

Amen.

- FRIDAY 9 -
Groans

Some days we wake up with them,
maybe because of the way things are.

Some days they come upon us suddenly,
maybe because of some particular event or person.

Some days they are with us all day long,
maybe because of the cumulative effect of experience in the world.

Groans.

They come from the exasperation or pain or frustration or impatience or longing we feel because of the difference—and sometimes it is a huge difference—between the way things are and the way they should be; the difference between the way things are and the way things, in your time and through your grace, will be.

Our groans are symptomatic, in other words.

Help us, Lord, to focus not on the groans themselves, not on the symptoms, but rather on the underlying causes.

Give us the hope and faith we need to look toward the new heaven and new earth for which our spirits and all of creation join in longing.

Give us the courage and initiative to direct our energies and efforts toward doing what we can to effect what change we can to make things better in this old earth, in the here and now, especially for those who are most without help and hope.

Give us the wisdom and compassion not to accept our groans as submissions to the way things are, but rather to view them as calls to trust and as calls to action.

Amen.

- FRIDAY 10 -
Children

Bless the children, O Lord.

Form them in the image of Christ.

Lead them to the best life they can have.

Help them to learn of you and to learn all else they need to know.

Give them a great sense of the basic unity of humankind and a lesser sense of the divisions we have created and perpetuated.

Grant them a desire for peace that will cause them to work for a better world.

Empower them to be

givers more than takers,
sharers more than hoarders,
makers more than consumers.

Let them be children even though so many of them are faced with way too much way too soon.

Protect and deliver those children who are or who could be victims of neglect or abuse.

Bless all those who are related to or work directly with children, Lord—parents, grandparents, teachers, counselors, ministers, Sunday school teachers, after-school program staffers, daycare workers, and others. Would you through your Spirit fill them with grace and love and wisdom and compassion, and would you cause them to be excellent role models?

Bless and cause to grow and never to die the childlikeness within us adults so that we might always acknowledge, celebrate, and live in our dependence on you so that we will constantly look to you for what we need to make it in this world and the next.

Amen.

- FRIDAY 11 -

Abilities

Whatever abilities we have come from you, so even as we thank you for them we must ask for protection from at least two sins.

The first sin is the sin of pride that can lead us to think more of ourselves and our abilities than we should, given that we did nothing to get them or to deserve them.

Such pride stunts gratitude to you and stifles humility toward ourselves and lessens appreciation for the abilities of others.

The second sin is the sin of irresponsibility that can lead us to fail to use and to continue to develop the abilities you have given us, given we did nothing to get them or to deserve them.

Such irresponsibility indicates a failure to comprehend your grace and an unwillingness to fill the gap in the world that is ours to fill.

So help us, Lord, to acknowledge with great joy the abilities that by your grace you have given us, and help us to be disciplined in the practice of those abilities so that they might be used as fully as possible for the good of your kingdom and for the good of the world always in a spirit of service, of sacrifice, and of love.

Amen.

- FRIDAY 12 -

Humble

It's not that we are worthless, that we are of no account—really it's not.

After all, the good God made us and the same good God loved us enough to send Jesus to die for us.

And, in Christ, God gives us the grace to become not better, but rather more—more like Christ, more in the image of Christ—which means at least that we become more and more who God from the beginning intended us to be.

It's good that we realize that!
It's good that we know that!

But that good thing, like all good things, comes with a dark side and with a possible down side that can be summarized in the word "pride."

It is so easy, as we realize that in Christ we are becoming more, for us to think we are becoming more than we in fact are.

And before we know it, we think more of ourselves and less of others than we ought; we spend more of our time and energy on ourselves and less on others than we ought; we talk more and listen less than we ought.

Forgive us, Lord, for thinking less of ourselves than we should and for thinking more of ourselves than we should.

Help us, Lord, to be humble in the right and best sense of the word so that we might live well before you and with each other.

Amen.

- FRIDAY 13 -
The Good Life

O God, may today be a good day, a day of good—a day in which we will live the good life.

May it be a day at the end of which we can look back and know we offered good things—love, kindness, gentleness, forgiveness, patience, mercy, understanding, time—to the people we encountered.

May it be a day at the end of which we can look back and know we received good things—grace, faith, hope, perseverance, endurance, perspective—from you.

We pray not for the ease that passes as the good life, but rather for the faithfulness in the midst of all circumstances that really is the good life.

Amen.

- FRIDAY 14 (OR GOOD FRIDAY) -

The Cross

Cause us today to see as we have never seen before

Jesus, betrayed;
Jesus, denied;
Jesus, abused;
Jesus, condemned;
Jesus, mocked;
Jesus, crucified;
Jesus, dead.

Cause us today to see as we have never seen before

our sin,
our responsibility,
our brokenness,
our need,
our mortality,
our alienation,
our lostness.

Cause us today to see as we have never seen before that in the cross of Christ it somehow all comes together so that in his death we begin to find our life.

Amen.

- FRIDAY 15 -

Eternal Life

O God,

One difference between you and us is the way we experience time.

We are time-bound; we experience life as "now" and "then."
You are outside of and above time; to you, all of time is of a piece.

Such is our human condition as contrasted with your divine nature, but in you we need to and can get past our limitation, past our time-bound nature.

Help us to know and to live in light of our knowing that our life with you is not just a future reality that begins when we die, but that it is already taking place right now; that it is not only a future reality, but also a present reality.

Help us to know and to live in light of our knowing that you are with us now, that we can experience a little bit of heaven now, and that our eternal life is already being experienced now.

Help us to know and to live in light of our knowing you and your Son, Jesus Christ our Lord—today.

Amen.

- FRIDAY 16 -
Kindness

We need more kindness, Lord, more simple, basic, human kindness.

Since kindness begins with awareness, please increase our awareness

of the presence of the other,
of the kinship of the other,
of the frailty of the other,
of the need of the other.

As we grow in our awareness of the other, please cause us to feel kindly toward each other and to act kindly toward each other.

Deliver us from cruelty that is so obviously wrong.
Deliver us from apathy that is closer to cruelty than it is to kindness.

In the end it matters how we have seen each other and how we have been toward each other.

So fill us with kindness, Lord, so that it flows from us and all over every person we encounter.

Amen.

- FRIDAY 17 -
Is

"It is what it is," they say.

It also is when it is. And when it is, is now.

The past, regardless of its value for educational purposes and of its potential production of regret and guilt, is the past.

The future, regardless of its value for inspiration and of its potential prompting of anxiety and fear, is the future.

It is the present that is, and it is in the present that we are.

O Lord, grant that we will

live in the here and now;
invest ourselves fully and give ourselves totally to this moment;
see each moment of life as the blessing it is; and
keep our eyes, our ears, and our spirits wide open in each moment.

You are outside of time, but we are not; help us to revel in the blessing of our limitation.

Amen.

- FRIDAY 18 -
Related

At the molecular level we are related to absolutely everything that exists in this world, whether it's a bird or a frog or a monkey or a rock—or another person.

Families of course have their squabbles, and so we don't always get along well with our relations.

The "things" in the world and we become estranged, sometimes at the instigation of the things—as in a natural disaster—but more often at our instigation—as in the harm we habitually inflict on our environment.

Forgive us, Lord, for the role we play in the drama of estrangement between nature and us. Help us to be and to do better.

We become estranged from our closest relations, too—namely other people—and the most likely and most painful estrangements are those from the closest relations among our closest relations—namely our family and friends and sisters and brothers in faith.

Forgive us, Lord, for the role we play in the drama of estrangement between other people and us. Help us to be and to do better.

Make us faithful in our relationships with everything and with everyone to whom we are related.

Amen.

- FRIDAY 19 -

Age

I am in my 50s. Others are in their teens, their 20s, their 30s, 40s, 50s, 60s, 70s, 80s, 90s—and a few even make it past 100.

If and when we are adults, we usually try to act our age—which is as it should be. When we don't act our age, it embarrasses us—which is usually as it should be.

Help us, Lord, to act our age, to be who we should be at our point in life.

We also have a faith age; we are at whatever stage of maturity in our faith we have, by your grace and our discipline, managed to attain.

Sometimes our growth is stunted so that our faith age is not what it should or could be; we find ourselves still demanding milk and cookies when vegetables should be on the daily menu.

Help us, Lord, to grow in faith and grace and love as we should so that, when we act our faith age, we will honor you and bear effective witness to the presence of Christ in our lives.

Yet there is one way in which we need to stay like little children: We need to keep on having the simple, childlike faith that trusts in you wholeheartedly as our great and gracious Father and knows that you always hold us in your great and loving arms.

Help us, Lord, in that way, always to be children—and always to act our age.

Amen.

- FRIDAY 20 -
Opinions

Everyone has them, which is both a curse and a blessing.

It's a curse

because differences of opinion can become a source of conflict;
because our egos can get wrapped up in our opinions so that being right becomes too important to us—even more important than being loving;
because our opinions can become so vital to us that we won't pay attention to facts that should adjust or even negate our opinions.

It's a blessing

because different perspectives can produce a more complete version of the truth;
because differences of opinion, when graciously held, can lead to helpful and constructive dialogue;
because differences of opinion, when freely and lovingly shared and heard, can lead to an increased respect for one another and to an increased sense of community.

O God, we thank you for the minds with which we can think and process and decide, our ability to form opinions and for the ability to change our minds, and for the presence of others from whose opinions we can learn and who can learn from ours.

Help us to submit our minds and our mouths—and, where appropriate, our pens and our keyboards—to you so that the forming and expressing of our opinions might be part of the solution and not part of the problem.

Amen.

- FRIDAY 21 -

Potential

More is in us that needs to come out and much of what has already come out needs to be better developed.

We all have a long way to go.
We all have much good we can do along the way.
We all have more in us than we will ever use.

Lord, thank you for our potential.

Please help us to realize it and to actualize it.

And help us to help others to realize and to actualize theirs.

Please don't let us waste what you have in your grace placed in us.

Amen.

- FRIDAY 22 -

Dance

Lord, you gifted some of us with a sense of rhythm; you gifted some of us with a willingness to give ourselves over to the moment with great abandon.

Others of us you did not so gift; still others of us may have been given those gifts but long ago buried them or had them buried for us.

Some of us, therefore, gladly dance while others of us will not dance gladly or otherwise.

Whether we dance so that everyone can see us doesn't matter much, but we all need the ability and the willingness to dance so that you can see us and so that we can know—at least deep down in inside—we are indeed dancing.

O Lord, please give us the spirit of dancing; give us a sense of joy and celebration over all the good gifts of this good life and especially over the great grace you have shown and continue to show us.

Cause us, at least in our hearts, to dance before you, because we need and want you to know that we celebrate you.

Amen.

- FRIDAY 23 -
Joke

Sometimes, amidst the absurdity of it all, it can feel like the joke is on us.

And maybe it is.

What if money and material things really aren't the key to a happy life?

What if working all the time really doesn't deepen our humanity?

What if being in charge really doesn't make us important?

What if being right really is less valuable than being kind?

What if being guided by grace really is better than following all the rules?

What if feeding the hungry and housing the homeless and saving the children really is more central to the righteous life than having the fine points of theology down pat?

What if this really isn't all there is?

What if God really does love us and accept us and forgive us and save us?

O God, through your Son and by your Spirit and in your Book you have let us in on the joke.

Grant that we not be, when all is said and done, the punch line.

Amen.

- FRIDAY 24 -
Patience

Sometimes it is good to be assertive and aggressive, to try to make things happen.

But sometimes, Lord, in pushing hard to move ahead we get outside of your timing.

Sometimes we need to take a deep breath, to trust, and to wait.

Grant us an active patience, oh Lord—a patience that waits on you but that is willing to act when the time seems right.

At the same time, cause us to undertake patient actions, Lord, so that even as we act we are not frenzied but are careful in listening for your guidance.

Make our patience active.
Make our actions patient.

Amen.

- FRIDAY 25 -
Vanity

The biblical word "vanity" has the root meaning of "breath" or "vapor" and thus came to mean "emptiness" or "nothingness." So when the Bible warns us against vanity, it is putting us on alert lest we attribute too much value to things that pass away like a vapor.

The problem is that some of the things in life that tempt us most toward vanity seem so solid, so physical: looks, money, houses, cars, and clothes, for example, are all so here, so present, and so real.

And yet the truth is that they will all pass away like a vapor even if the decomposition process takes a while.

Surely, though, some of the things that are most substantial and valuable are experienced in our physical lives—relationships, for example, especially family relationships, but other significant ones, too.

Maybe an important difference between things like relationships and things like looks is that things like relationships have a spiritual—and thus a more personal—component to them, so maybe they have some staying power that vain things don't. Maybe things like relationships last.

O Lord, guard us against vanity; keep us from giving much weight to things that are inevitably going to float away.

But Lord, help us to value appropriately those things in life that do have weight and that do have staying power.

It is hard to say which is sadder: to value that which is not ultimately valuable or to devalue that which is.

Give us the wisdom to do neither.

Amen.

- FRIDAY 26 -
Sharing

Help us, O God, to share our stuff, our possessions, our things, our bounty with people who need it. Much of the joy and meaning in life is found, after all, in how we give out of that with which you have blessed us.

Help us even more, O God, to share our lives, ourselves, with others. After all, our selves are our most unique and valuable possession, and it is in sharing them that we get to the heart of the matter; it is in sharing them that we truly give ourselves away.

Keep us aware of the truth that our openness, our vulnerability, our friendship, our grace, may just be someone's lifeline.

Help us to share ourselves for that person's sake, for our own sake, and even, since we serve a God whose character is seen most clearly in the Son who gave his life away, for your sake.

Amen.

- FRIDAY 27 -
Saved

To say we are saved is to say we are in need of rescue.

Isn't that the truth!

O God, each of us has our own particular bondage, our own particular variation on the power we call "sin," and without your grace we remain in that bondage.

But in Christ you have set us free, you are setting us free, and you will set us free.

Thank you, God, for saving us; thank you for setting us free.

Help us to grow in our salvation today and every day.

Amen.

- FRIDAY 28 -
The Roll

"When the roll is called up yonder, I'll be there." I have sung it a thousand times and I confess that I do, with great faith in the grace of God, believe it.

It occurs to me, though, how long that roll is getting. Sometimes it feels like I know more people who are on the roll up yonder than are in my address book down here.

I reckon the older I get, the more like that it's naturally going to seem.

Thank you, Lord, for all the people I've had the great privilege of knowing.

Thank you, Lord, for the ones who are now with you and for the joy they know.

Thank you, Lord, for the ways in which they live on as well in the memories I and others have.

Thank you, Lord, that the great community you are establishing now will continue then, forever.

Thank you, Lord, that there is a roll—a Book of Life—in which the names of all your family members are listed.

Cause us to rest confidently in your grace.

Amen.

- FRIDAY 29 -
Right

Help us today, O Lord, to live right in the right way.

It is possible, after all, for us to live right in the wrong way.

We can, for example, do the right things for the wrong reasons, such as to gain the admiration of people or to build ourselves up in your eyes or to make ourselves feel better about ourselves or to compensate outwardly for what we fear is terribly wrong inwardly.

Help us to grow out of and to progress away from motives that come from self-centeredness.

It is also possible, though, for us to live right in the right way.

We can, with your help, do the right thing for the right reasons, such as to respond to your love with our love, to forgive because we have been forgiven, to help and to serve with no thought of reward, and to live out of a maturing faith—one mark of which is a failure to think our faith is all that mature.

Help us to grow into and to progress toward motives that come from love of you and love of others.

It is possible for us to live right but to be insufferable in so doing.

Cause us rather, Lord, to live right and to be gracious in so doing.

Amen.

- FRIDAY 30 -
Tapestry

Sometimes you have the opportunity to be in a place where you are around people from all over the planet.

In that situation you see all kinds of faces, you hear all kinds of languages, you see all kinds of clothing, and you experience all kinds of cultures.

When that happens, you can hardly help but be amazed at the beautiful tapestry God has in grace and love woven in this world.

Thank you, God, for the way I look and talk and dress and live.

Thank you, God, for the ways others look and talk and dress and live.

Help us to see how you have woven us into a beautiful tapestry, and help us to celebrate—and to continue to develop—your beautiful human creation.

May we live in ways that will strengthen and extend your weaving, and not in ways that will contribute to its unraveling.

Amen.

- FRIDAY 31 -
Attention

Thank you, Lord, for the ability to concentrate, to pay attention to that to which attention needs to be paid.

Increase our ability—and our willingness—to pay attention to what is important.

In particular, help us to pay greater attention

to you and to what you are up to all around us,
to our own spirits and to what is growing or festering in them,
to other people and to their hopes and dreams and needs.

At the same time, increase our ability—and our willingness—to pay less attention to what is unimportant.

In particular, help us to pay less attention

to the biases and prejudices birthed by our fears,
to the consumerism birthed by our greed and lust,
to the narrow-mindedness birthed by our particular context.

O God, help us to pay attention—or not to pay attention—in ways that will glorify you, that will ennoble us, and that will bless others.

Amen.

- FRIDAY 32 -
Devotion

When faced with trial or trouble or tragedy, we can abandon our devotion to God.

Or, we can continue to practice and even increase our devotion.

Or, we can promise in the face of such problems to grow in our devotion but, when things get better, forget our promise.

Or, we can become disoriented so that we fail to distinguish devotion from lack of devotion.

Lord God, help us to be devoted to you.

Help us to grow in our devotion to you so that when difficult times come —which they inevitably will—we will be ready to remain devoted.

Keep us from the presumption that makes it easy to be blindsided by events that would challenge our devotion.

And cause us to keep a close watch on our hearts so that we might evaluate our devotion accurately and take the appropriate steps to strengthen it.

Lord God, help us to be devoted to you.

Amen.

- FRIDAY 33 -
Cherished

I am cherished. You are cherished. All God's children are cherished. So everyone we see today, including the one each of us will see in the mirror, is cherished.

Let us celebrate the remarkable fact that God not only thinks of us, but also when God thinks of us the thought God thinks is a thought of love.

Thank you, God, for the amazing grace that inspires you to cherish us.

Help us to know and to live in the light of your creation of us, your acceptance of us, your love for us, your embrace of us, and your cherishing of us.

Cause us to treat everyone we meet today in light of the fact that you cherish them.

You cherish us, so we can and we will rest in you.

Amen.

- FRIDAY 34 -
Suffering

Thank you, God, for the ability to feel suffering and for the blessing, when it comes, of feeling it.

To affirm that suffering can be a blessing is not to fall prey to some extreme postures that can inflict unnecessary suffering on ourselves and on others.

So protect us from a masochism that would cause us to seek suffering for ourselves and to find pleasure in it. And protect us from a sadism that would cause us to seek to inflict suffering on others and to find pleasure in that.

At the same time, guard us against a desire to avoid or to deny the suffering that comes to us in the course of living or that comes to us in the course of trying to be faithful in our service to you and to others. Guard us also against the tendencies to compare the suffering others experience to what we experience and to dismiss theirs in light of ours or to fail to help to tend to theirs because we have to tend to ours.

Help us, Lord, to see our suffering—whether it be physical, emotional, mental, or spiritual—as an opportunity to find common ground with the rest of suffering humanity and as a chance for your grace and love to enter us anew through the break that occurs in our hearts when we suffer.

When some particular suffering ceases, help us not to forget its lessons.

When some particular suffering endures, help us to keep on learning its lessons.

Amen.

- FRIDAY 35 -
Adventure

Thank you, God, for the adventure today is. It is an adventure because it is uncharted territory; it is a journey through a time we have never experienced before.

Oh, there will be routine in it, to be sure, and there will be people we see every day and things we do every day, but still, there will be differences in the routine and the same old people, and the same old things will have a different twist to them because they have changed since yesterday—and we have changed since yesterday —if only in very small ways.

So give us a sense of excitement about the adventure that is today.

Give us courage to face what we must face.

Give us faith to go where we've never gone before.

Give us the ability to see with new eyes this new day with its new possibilities.

Today is a day we have never had before and we will never have again.

Cause us to embrace with an adventurous spirit the adventure this day is.

Amen.

- FRIDAY 36 -
After

On the one hand, we are guaranteed no moment beyond the one in which we are taking our current breath; on the other hand, odds are we have a few more moments—if not hours or days or years or even decades—coming after this moment.

So Lord, give us the peace that comes from accepting the facts that (a) we may have no future; and (b) if we do, then there's no way to know what will happen in it so there's no advantage in worrying about it; and (c) whether we die or whether we live, our lives are in your hands.

At the same time, give us the hope that comes from accepting the facts that (a) just as all our previous moments have prepared us for the living of this one, so does this moment prepare us for the living of our future moments; and (b) while the choices we make and others make have a lot to say about the directions our future might take, your grace has an even louder voice; and (c) whether we die or whether we live, our lives are in your hands.

Help us, O God, to live fully in this moment; help us to live it with the peace and hope that come from knowing all our moments are wrapped up in your grace.

Amen.

- FRIDAY 37 -
Kind of

"I'm kind of tired."
"I'm kind of angry."
"I'm kind of confused."
"I'm kind of resentful."
"I'm kind of nice."
"I'm kind of reliable."
"I'm kind of forgiving."
"I'm kind of loving."
"I'm kind of ready."

We say things like that because we are things like that.

When we say things like that we mean we are more or less that way, that we are to some extent that way, that we are rather that way.

So when we talk like that we are confessing we are not complete or perfect—or we are not completely imperfect—and we are acknowledging the truth that we have not yet arrived—but that neither are we still, or at least not quite, where we started.

There are, in other words, places in our lives where we are something and we aren't that same something—at the same time.

Lord, we admit we are only "kind of" everything we are.

Deliver us from blind spots that would cause us to think we are fully and completely what we should be—which results in arrogance—or to think we are fully and completely what we shouldn't be—which results in despair.

Cause us to embrace our incompleteness with hope and trust that you are by your grace working in those places where we simultaneously are and aren't to form us more into who we will be.

Amen.

- FRIDAY 38 -
Quotation Marks

We employ quotation marks to denote we are repeating what someone else said; indeed, to put a statement within quotation marks is to assert we are repeating their words exactly. Sometimes we do so explicitly in writing, and sometimes we do so implicitly in talking.

There is potentially both good and bad in such repeating.

Lord, guard us from the too-easy acceptance of and parroting of what others say—particularly if they are confirming our prejudices—and the habit of being part of a chain that passes along what someone supposedly said—whether we are the first link in the chain and thus have some chance of getting it right or a link farther down the chain and have every chance of getting it wrong.

Lord, lead us toward the sayings and observations of people whose quotes serve to build up and not to tear down, to heal and not to kill, to help and not to hurt and, as appropriate, to challenge and not to affirm or to affirm and not to challenge. Lead us toward the discipline of repeating other people's words in ways that show appropriate honor and respect for them as persons who have been created by you and whose lives and reputations and families matter.

Give us integrity in the ways we hear and in the ways we repeat.

Amen.

- FRIDAY 39 -
The Name

In Bible times a person's name summarized who that person was; to reveal your name to someone was to tell them something of who you were. Moreover, to give someone your name was to give them the ability to use your name in blessings and in curses and so to put you to some degree at the disposal of that person.

To take someone's name in vain was to treat it as if it was of no weight and importance or to use it for wrong or improper purposes.

God in the Bible revealed God's self in many names. But the primary ones are "Yahweh," which means something like "I am who I am," and "Jesus," which means something like "The Lord saves." So those main names reveal some important truths about God.

O God, help us not to take your name in vain, not to use it for wrong purposes, and not to treat it lightly or as of little importance.

Help us not

to speak of you as if you are less than Almighty God;
to employ your name to get our own way or to further our own agenda;
to live, as people who bear your family name, in ways that bring disrespect to that name;

to pray in ways that treat your name as a talisman that helps us get what we want rather than as the essence of the One to whose will and way we want to submit.

Help us

to speak of you carefully and reverently as befits Almighty God;
to tell the truth as it befits those who, whether they directly invoke it or not, are always speaking in your name;
to live as people who not only bear your name, but also who know you personally and who, because we love you and are committed to you, want accurately to reflect your character to those around us;
to remember that, because you have revealed yourself to us, especially in the person of Jesus, we can with some confidence know if what we are doing or saying or promoting or resisting is in line with who you are but that at the same time, because you are God, we should maintain a healthy humility about such things.

Amen.

- FRIDAY 40 -
Truth

O Lord,

The words we speak affect people and situations and events and perceptions and processes and outcomes.

When we speak, let our words

build up and not tear down;
help and not hurt;
contribute to the solution and not to the problem;
be humble and not arrogant;
be true and not false.

Guard our hearts out of which our words come because it is far too easy for us to spin the truth in line with our preconceived notions or in order to promote our self-focused agenda.

Cause us to speak the truth.
Empower us to speak the truth in love.
Enable us, when it is best—and it often is—to keep the truth in silence.

Amen.

- FRIDAY 41 -
Beauty

Beauty is in the eye of the beholder, they say.

Since you made us, O Lord, you must behold us all as beautiful.

Help us, then, to see ourselves—and everyone else—through your eyes.

Amen.

- FRIDAY 42 -
Everywhere

Right now the place where I find myself is "here."
And you, O God, are with me here.

Other destinations and situations lie in my future, so at some point I will be "there."
And you, O God, will be with me there.

Thank you, O God, that you are with me everywhere, that there is no place I can go apart from your presence.

Heighten my spiritual senses so that I may be perpetually aware of your perpetual presence—so that I may be in every way aware that you are with me everywhere.

Amen.

- FRIDAY 43 -
Priests

When we put a mental label on ourselves to name what we are, "priest" is not the first word to come to mind; it may not even be the last.

We have the job, though, whether we want it or not, since your Book tells us that because of the saving work of Jesus Christ all who trust in him are priests with priestly privileges and priestly responsibilities.

Help us, Lord, to want the job.

Help us to want to celebrate and to take advantage of the privilege of direct access to you; help us to practice the disciplines of prayer and Bible study and worship that will keep the way between you and us wide open.

Help us to want to accept and to exercise the responsibility of being a priest to others, of living in such a way that other people will see Jesus in us and will want to come to know the Christ who has made all the difference to us.

Thank you, Lord, for our priesthood. May we live it out in ways that generate wholeness and integrity in us that will be pleasing to you and appealing to others.

Amen.

- FRIDAY 44 -

Death/Life

Jesus said to his disciples, including Thomas, "Lazarus is dead. For your sake I am glad I was not there, so that you may believe. Let us go to him." Thomas then said to the other disciples, "Let us also go, that we may die with him."

Often, we get what we are looking for.

If we expect to find despair and death, we are not disappointed.
If we expect to find hope and life, we are also not disappointed.

It's not really about attitude, though; it's about reality, and the reality is that where Jesus, who is the resurrection and the life, is we can legitimately expect and anticipate that despair will give way to hope and death will give way to life.

Others have testified to that reality.
We have experienced that reality ourselves.

O God, in a world filled with despair rooted in death, empower us with hope that is rooted in life. Cause us to be so aware of the presence of our resurrected Lord that we live in constant expectation of life and that we will die with a bold trust in everlasting life.

Thomas had it right in a way. We are called to die with Jesus, to be crucified with him, to take up our cross and follow him, to lose our lives for his sake.

But on the other side of death, be it death to self or death to earthly life, there is in our risen Lord resurrection and life.

Thanks be to God!

Amen.

- FRIDAY 45 -
You

It is with you, O God, that I have to deal—and for reasons I confess I don't quite understand.

You are God, after all, so why should you care about me, much less love me?

But you do, and I am astounded.

My life is but one among billions, so why should you poke and prod and nudge and shove and pull and yank me along as if who I become and what I do matters?

But you do, and I am astounded.

If not for you and your determination to be known by me, I could not know you.

You cause my awareness of you.
You prompt my consciousness of you.
You inspire my love of you.
You forgive my sins against you.
You grace my efforts for you.
You embrace my life in you.

It is with you that I have to deal, O God—and it is all because of who you are.
Thanks be to you!

Amen.

- FRIDAY 46 -

Lift

Sometimes we need a lift, Lord, and it's more than a boost in our spirits when we get a little downhearted that we need.

The problem is that sometimes we can't see over whatever is in front of us; what's there might or might not be something big—it's just that it's so close, it fills our field of vision and dominates our attention.

And so we need a lift to see over it; we need a lift so we can get a glimpse of the other side and thus expand our vision to include just a little bit of hope—just a little bit.

We don't ask that you take it away; we don't ask for it to be dealt with without our taking appropriate responsibility for it.

We just ask that by your grace and mercy and great love you lift us up just enough—just barely enough.

Amen.

- FRIDAY 47 -

Categories

Lord, save us from the mistake of categorizing people.

Stop our tongue if ever we begin to speak a sentence that begins with or includes words such as "they all" or "all of them." Guard us from the false witness to which such a sentence inevitably leads.

Well, except for a sentence like "They all are loved by God, so all of them should be loved by me."

Amen.

- FRIDAY 48 -
Unsettled

We feel unsettled; it may be

because of the way the world is or
because of the way people are or
because of the way we are or
because of the way I am or
because of the way you are, O God.

Or maybe it's because of the way it all is all the time.

Lord, when the unsettledness gets in the way, when it becomes a distraction, when it tilts toward dysfunction, then settle us down and increase our peace.

But Lord, when we get to feeling too settled or too at ease, when our serenity results from inattention, then unsettle us and increase our awareness.

And Lord, cause our unsettledness to be for us the place where you work on us to bring about change and creativity through which we might do something where something needs to be done about the way things are; the place where you work on us to bring about acceptance through which we learn to accept the way things are where things need to be left alone.

Amen.

- FRIDAY 49 -
Story

We each have a story; I have the story of me, you have the story of you, she has the story of her, and he has the story of him.

We all have a story; we have the story of us; the human race has a story, and the various groupings—family, tribe, clan, ethnic group, nation—within humanity have a story.

Thank you, God, for our stories. Thank you for their high points and low points; thank you for their victories and defeats; thank you for their joys and sorrows; thank you for their gains and losses; thank you for their pleasures and pains. Thank you for the privilege of living my story and of living our story.

You have a story, too, O God—a story you are living out, a story in which you in your grace give us a part, a story in which you in your grace sometimes participate right here on our part of the stage in ways that make you hard to miss.

Jesus comes to mind.
So do some moments in our own lives.

Keep us aware, O God, that our stories are a part of your story,

a story of which you are the author—although you let us do some of the writing,

a story of which you are the director—although you let us do a lot of improvising,

a story in which you are the lead actor—although you give us important supporting roles.

Give us faith and grace to live the story for all it's worth.

Amen.

- FRIDAY 50 -
Recount

To recount something is to describe an event or an occurrence in detail.
To recount something is also to count it again.

Help us, God, to follow the model of the psalmists who recounted your great saving acts on behalf of your people—who named and described them, who left us their namings and descriptions of them so that we might be able to go over them again and again and so that we might be inspired to describe your saving acts on our behalf and to go over them again and again.

Forgive us, God, for having to be reminded to recount all you have done, are doing, and will do for us.

But do remind us to count our many blessings—and to recount them and recount them and recount them.

Amen.

- FRIDAY 51 (OR CHRISTMAS EVE) -

Eve

The eve of a day is the day before that day; it is the day on which we can finally say of that day to which we have been looking forward and toward which we have been pointing for so long, "It is tomorrow."

It is a day on which we are on the edge, on the verge, on the brink, on the precipice.

It is a day on which we are filled with energy and excitement that result from almost fulfilled expectation and from barely contained anticipation.

It is a day on which our senses are heightened and our emotions are sharpened and our thoughts are focused.

It is a day, then, that can remind us of what all of our days should be like—if to a more limited degree than on this particular eve, in order to preserve our sanity—given that we are always on the eve of the coming of the Son to us in new and challenging and different and surprising ways.

Teach us on this eve, O God, something of how to live in constant expectation and anticipation of the coming of your Son to us.

Amen.

- FRIDAY 52 -

Faithfulness

Thank you, God, that it has been true this year.
Thank you, God, that it will be true next year.

Amen.

Saturday Prayers

- SATURDAY 1 -
Discernment

Many words will come my way today,

some from talking people,
some from printed pages,
some from glowing screens,
some from my own wandering mind and thundering imagination.

Grant me the gift of discernment, O Lord, so that I may know

the good from the bad,
the true from the false,
the helpful from the hurtful,
the constructive from the destructive,
the benevolent from the self-serving,
the useful from the manipulative;
the information from the noise.

Above all, O Lord, grant me the discernment to recognize those words that are the best words—the ones that are your words—wherever I may hear them.

Amen.

- SATURDAY 2 -
Look

Help me, Lord, to look back—on this week, on this year, on my life
—so as to celebrate, to repent, to learn. But don't let me look back too long.

Help me, Lord, to look ahead—to tomorrow, to next year, to eternity
—so as to anticipate, to plan, to wonder. But don't let me look ahead too long.

Help me, Lord, to look down—to where I am, to who I'm with, to what I'm doing—so that I might be fully present and fully alive in this day, in this moment.

Amen.

- SATURDAY 3 -

Play

I hope I'll get to play in heaven
because I sure don't play much down here.

Forgive me, Lord,

for the anxiety that makes me think it will all fall apart without me,
for the arrogance that makes me always try to make things happen,
for the angst that makes me fill all my time and space with work.

Turn me, Lord,

toward trust that will compel me to let go,
toward humility that will lead me to let others,
toward peace that will allow me to let up.

There is so much good and helpful work to accomplish, Lord,
I want to stay at it all the time.

But there is so much to be enjoyed.
There is so much fun to be had.
There is so much playing to do.

I know you want me to.
Now help me to want to.

"Go outside and play," Mama said.

It was the word of the Lord.

Help me to hear it and to obey it now.

Amen.

- SATURDAY 4 -
Rest

We cannot always rest in the sense of stopping everything and doing nothing, but for those moments when we can, we thank you, Lord, and ask that in the stillness and quiet of such moments we will think of you and, having thought of you, we will praise you and ask you to cultivate in us a rest that is perpetual;

a rest that is always present down deep in our spirit, regardless of the frenzy going on around us and even sometimes within us;

a rest that knows we are always in your arms, the peace that passes understanding, an abiding trust in you, that you make your home with us;

a rest that is precursor to the everlasting rest that will be ours when we make our home with you.

Amen.

- SATURDAY 5 -
Places

For special places, O Lord, we thank you.

We thank you for places that are special to us because something happened there, or something started there, or something ended there, or something changed there, or something endures there.

Some of them are places to which we hope to return, while some of them are places to which we return with regularity, while others are places to which we return occasionally or rarely, while others are places to which we will never return.

In any case, we carry them in us as surely as they once carried us in them.

Even as we remember those special and powerful places of the past, O Lord, focus our attention on the special and powerful place of the future—the home toward which you are inexorably drawing us—and the special and powerful place of the present—the home we have right now.

Amen.

- SATURDAY 6 -
Forgiveness

Sometimes we dare to pray for a miracle, and there is no miracle greater than the miracle of forgiveness.

Thank you for the miracle that happens when you forgive us.
Thank you for the miracle that happens when we forgive someone.
Thank you for the miracle that happens when someone forgives us.
Thank you for the miracle that happens when we are able to accept forgiveness.

It is by grace, all by your grace.

So Lord, given the way things are—the way others are, the way we are, the way I am —we will need that miracle again today.

Let it be, dear Lord, let it be
—by your grace, all by your grace.

Amen.

- SATURDAY 7 -
Off

Sometimes "we're off"—which can mean several things.

"I'm off" means I am at the beginning of a trip or a project or an adventure.

"I'm off work" means I am not required to fulfill my normal vocational responsibilities.

"I'm off my game" means that things are not going as I think they should go and that I'm not quite as in control of my actions and of their outcomes as I usually think I am.

"I'm off my rocker" means I feel like I'm losing my mind..

Lord, enable us to see and to know that those times when we are off are moments when we can be and should be uncommonly and unusually open to your grace because they are times when, since the usual pattern and routine are not applicable, the mystery deepens and the wonder widens and the possibilities expand and we are more apt to be surprised and amazed over and attentive to your presence.

Amen.

- SATURDAY 8 -
Senses

Most of us have five of them; some of us have less, and all of us make less use than we could and should of the ones we have.

After all, our senses are all designed to take in the range of things, the extremes of things, and everything in between:

We taste the sweet and the bitter.
We smell the savory and the foul.
We touch the smooth and the rough.
We see the sightly and the unsightly.
We hear the soft and the harsh.

And we too easily assume that since things toward one end of the range are more immediately pleasant than things toward the other end, they are therefore better.

But that's not necessarily so.

So Lord, would you enable us to embrace the full range of our experiences so that we might not miss all you have to say to us in this life that you in your grace and love have given us to live.

Amen.

- SATURDAY 9 -

Re-creation

I believe in God, creator of heaven and earth.
I believe in God, creator of my life and of all lives.
I believe that God will someday re-create the heavens and the earth through Christ our Lord.
I believe that God will someday re-create my life and all lives through the resurrection of the dead.

Help me to believe, O God, and to live as if I believe, that you can and will re-create even now—even today—what is dead and dying in this world.

Help me to believe, O God, and to live as if I believe, that you can and will re-create even now—even today—what is dead and dying in me and in us.

Amen.

- SATURDAY 10 -

Stillness

"Be still" a parent says to a child who is being frenetic, whose activity or speaking or fretting seems on the verge of becoming perpetual.

"Be still" God says to me because I have not put away all childish ways.

Grant, O God, that I will be better disciplined in practicing stillness.

Help me to take time apart from everything—a time to be temporarily still.

Help me to nurture and tend to and remain in that place within me where your peace resides—a place to be perpetually still.

Grant, O God, through your grace, that in my set-apart time and in my set-apart place I will be still and know

who you are—that you are God;
who I am—that I am me;
whose I am—that I am yours.

Amen.

- SATURDAY 11 -

Enough

It is not enough to be nice, to be easygoing, to be passive.

Help us, Lord, not to settle.

It is not enough to love safely, to treat others well, to avoid doing wrong.

Help us, Lord, not to settle.

It may not even be enough to love as well as we can, to treat others as well as we can, to shun all the wrong we can.

If it's not, then help us, Lord, not to settle.

So what is enough?

It is enough to love with a radical sacrificial love that goes to the core of our being and that causes us always to seek what is best for the other.

It is enough to have such respect and honor for each other that we truly and deeply thrill to be in each other's presence and that we truly and deeply celebrate the good things that happen to the other.

It is enough that our hearts break so over the hurts we inflict and over the wrongs people inflict on themselves and on others that we must, empowered by your good and by your love, stand and fight against all such hurts and wrongs perpetrated against the other.

Help us, Lord, not to settle for anything less than your love, grace, and mercy taking such hold of us that we in our loving and in our living go far beyond that of which we are in our own right capable.

Amen.

- SATURDAY 12 -

Payback

Revenge is a delicacy that tastes sweet at first bite but that, upon chewing and swallowing, leaves a most bitter taste.

Maybe that's one of the causes of all the bitterness in the world; we're caught in a never-ending cycle of revenge. Sometimes we actively seek revenge; sometimes we lovingly nurture thoughts of revenge with no real intention of acting on them. But the bitterness remains and grows, affecting our attitudes and our actions.

Forgive us, Lord, when we want to or do repay evil with evil and thereby add to the already way-too-large pile of evil in this old world.

Empower us, Lord, to respond to evil with good, to sin with grace, and to hate with love and thereby to add to the sadly way-too-small piles of good, of grace, and of love in this old world.

Amen.

- SATURDAY 13 -

Routine

Thank you, Lord, for the daily routine.

As the rising and setting of the sun indicate the sameness and normalcy of each day, so do the routines of our daily lives give us a sense of order and security in each day.

Besides, if there was no routine there could be no surprises, no unexpected occurrences, no inbreakings. It is only in the sameness that we can experience and detect the difference.

So thank you, Lord, for the routine of the day in which there is much ongoing and expected grace. Thank you also for the disruptions of that routine in which there is much unexpected and surprising grace.

In both cases, please give us eyes that see and spirits that discern your grace.

Amen.

- SATURDAY 14 (OR HOLY SATURDAY) -

The Tomb

This is a day of grief.

As such, it is a day to which we can relate because

we all have known what it is to be wherever we are on the day after the funeral;

we all have known what it is to live with the shock and disbelief, with the sense of unreality, that are the aftermath of the death of a loved one;

we all have known what it is to see shattered the hopes and expectations we had attached to the person who is now in the grave.

Paul had not written about it yet and there is no indication the disciples understood yet what it meant to grieve with hope.

We do because on this dark Saturday we know about tomorrow—about Sunday.

We thank you, Lord, that the grief we feel today over our Lord in his tomb is etched with hope.

But we ask you, Lord, to cause us today to share deeply in the grief of those first followers of Jesus so that we might be fully aware of the fact of the very real death of the very real Jesus.

Amen.

- SATURDAY 15 -

Today

In some ways it's just another day; in other ways it's a day unlike any other.

Thank you for the expected and for the stability it brings; thank you for the unexpected and for the energy it produces.

Cause us, Lord, to see it all as grace; to approach it all as opportunity; to live it all as joy.

Amen.

- SATURDAY 16 -

Dirt

Thank you, Lord, for the dirt beneath our feet. Thank you for the blessing of working in it and through it and with it—with the result that we get to see other living things take root, grow up, and produce.

It must be something like the satisfaction you get from forming and then watching us. There is something about kneeling on the earth and digging down into the dirt with our hands; it feels like home.

Thank you for the opportunity to visit home.
Help us to tend it and to protect it and thus to value it.

There is also something about standing or sitting on the earth and gazing into the vastness of the night sky we cannot touch or visit or work in and that is thus far beyond us. Somewhere down inside us it feels like home, too.

And so it is that while we are at home, we also long for home.

Lord, make and keep us aware of who we are and of where we are.

Amen.

- SATURDAY 17 -

Will Be

On the one hand, "Whatever will be will be" sounds too deterministic and fatalistic.

On the other hand, "I can choose and make my own future" sounds presumptuous and egotistical.

Perhaps it comes down to the old question, "Does God really determine the future or do my choices really matter?" the answer to which appears to be "Yes."

Of this much we can be sure, Lord: We cannot see the future, and we certainly cannot live in it. So please forgive us for the time and energy we waste in fretting over it or in fantasizing about it.

Thank you for the teaching of your Word that you are, in all times and through all things, working your purposes out.

By your grace,

help us to live as much in line with those purposes as possible;
help us to make the best choices we can, since different paths do lead to different places along the way;
help us to be faithful to you and to others and to leave the outcomes to you.

Amen.

- SATURDAY 18 -
The Main Things

Thank you, Lord.
Forgive me, Lord.
Help me, Lord.

Amen.

- SATURDAY 19 -
Behind

We don't have eyes in the back of our heads, which means if we want to see what is behind us, we must make the effort to turn around and look.

It is good for us to remember that fact so that we will remember occasionally to make the effort.

Otherwise, we will fall prey to the delusion that the only reality is the one in front of us.

Remind us, Lord, that there is always another side, another perspective, another angle from which to view reality.

Prompt us, O God, to turn around and see what is behind us.

Amen.

- SATURDAY 20 -

Get Down

It's one of those phrases that can mean seemingly disparate things.

When we "get down,"
we're becoming depressed.

When we "get down,"
we're having a good time.

When we "get down" to it,
we're getting to work.

When we "get down" to it,
we're focusing on the essence of things.

Perhaps the essence of things is that life involves

having bad times,
having good times,
having a purpose.

So, Lord, for all the ways we "get down" in life, we thank you.

And in all the ways we "get down" in life, help us to praise you and to serve you and to remember that, when we get down to it, we can find meaning and faith and grace and hope in all of it.

Amen.

- SATURDAY 21 -

Heroes

For all of those who gave themselves up to help make me who I am, I thank you.

For the grace to give myself up to help others become who you mean them to be,
I ask you.

Amen.

- SATURDAY 22 -
Excess

A lot of people have an excess of money and material things
—they have way more than they need.

Such people also have an excess of the ability to share and to help in material ways.

A lot of people have an excess of poverty and scarcity
—they have way more than they should.

Such people also can have an excess of the ability to trust and to hope in the face of want and insecurity.

It is hard not to see how, if we would all bring our excesses together and share out of them, we would not all come away with more of what we really need.

Help us, Lord, to be willing to share out of our excess and then to do so, and in doing so to build community with you and with each other.

Amen.

- SATURDAY 23 -
Knowledge

We all know a lot about a lot—or maybe a little about a lot and a lot about a little.

Help us, Lord, to put such knowledge to good use, to use it to do good and to make things better.

Help us to use it to build up and not to tear down, to help and not to hinder, to heal and not to hurt.

Cause us to put our knowledge to good use for your sake, for our sake, for the world's sake, and for the Kingdom's sake.

Amen.

- SATURDAY 24 -

Quicken

It's an old Bible word that means to be made alive.

Lord God, please quicken us.

After all, there is, unfortunately and paradoxically, so much in our daily living that threatens to deaden us—pain, grief, discouragement, fear, and anxiety, just to name a few realities that can drain the life out of us.

The resurrection of Jesus Christ, though, means that none of the experiences that deaden us—not even death itself—have the final word or claim the final victory.

Dear Lord, through the life of your resurrected Son, quicken us. Give us life even in the midst of the worst circumstances we face.

And having been quickened, cause us to use our lives to worship, to love, and to serve you by sharing life in and with this world that all too often seems to have death hanging over it like a shroud and so could use a little quickening.

Amen.

- SATURDAY 25 -

Wonder

We use the word in two main ways: "I wonder what's going to happen" and "I am filled with wonder before Almighty God." In both cases we are affirming there is much we don't know and expressing some amazement over the possibilities.

O God, keep us filled with wonder as we face the future and as we seek your face. Forgive us for our sometimes arrogance that causes us to live as if we know the way before us or as if we know you more fully than we do; living that way cuts us off from wonder and from much of the thrill of living.

Give us rather a growing sense of wonder that will lead to a growing sense of humility, of hope, of trust, and of excitement.

Amen.

- SATURDAY 26 -

Lives

Along the way we enter into the lives of people and they into ours.

In some cases, the entering turns into remaining: We enter into so as to remain in the lives of our parents, our spouses, our children, and our lifelong friends, for example.

In other cases, the entering leads to visiting: We enter into so as to stay for just a little while in the lives of those we meet but never see again, those we are with for a few days but not in an ongoing way, and those we partner with for a particular purpose but not after the purpose is fulfilled, for example.

In either case, as well as in cases in between those two extremes, though, life touches life and—when life touches life—lives are changed.

O Lord, make us open to each other, vulnerable with each other, gracious to each other, and loving toward each other so that, as life touches life, both lives will be better and both lives will be blessed.

Amen.

- SATURDAY 27 -

Clarity

It is probably good that clarity comes to us so seldom because it is in making our way through the mists—through the vagaries and uncertainties and mysteries—of life that we are forced to trust and to try and to be creative.

Seeing dimly forces us to find ways to focus.

But every great once in a while, the mist lifts for just a moment and we catch a very clear and real glimpse of the way things really are, of the way we really are in your eyes, and—miracle of miracles—of the way you are with us and for us.

The moment passes.

But while it lasts we are filled with grace and peace and love—and gratitude—in which we can plunge back into the mists of our living.

Such a moment of clarity can make a day, a week, a year—even a life.

Thanks be to God.

Amen.

- SATURDAY 28 -

Travel

Unless they are homebound for reasons of health, everyone travels; everyone from time to time—and maybe lots of the time—leaves where they are in order to get somewhere else.

Whether it's a trip to the grocery store or a journey to the other side of the world, it requires travel.

On the one hand, travel is good and healthy and fun and can even, depending on the scenery along the way, be glorious.

On the other hand, travel is time-consuming and resource-consuming and can even, depending on circumstances and our level of carefulness—and that of other travelers—be dangerous.

But it's probably less dangerous to our perspective and our balance and our growth than staying put.

Give us, O God, traveling opportunities.
Grant us, O God, traveling mercies.

And may we learn as we travel something about the ways we should live
—which are, after all, quite a trip themselves.

Amen.

- SATURDAY 29 -
Gratitude

We are grateful to you, God, for

the air we breathe,
the water we drink,
the food we eat,
the friends we cherish,
the family we love,
the obstacles we face,
the tests we endure,
the victories we know,
the defeats we suffer,

and, in all things...the grace we experience.

We are grateful to you, God, in short, for our lives and for your help in living them. Inspire us to live with a spirit of gratitude.

Amen.

- SATURDAY 30 -
Give

We thank you, O God, for those who have given of themselves and who do give of themselves for the sake of others.

We thank you for their selflessness and their grace and their love.

We thank you for anyone who puts the needs of others ahead of the needs of self.

We thank you especially for Jesus Christ our Lord who loved us and gave himself for us, who came not to be served but to serve and to give his life as a ransom for many, and who emptied himself, taking the form of a servant.

May we who follow him love like he loved and give like he gave.

Give us the grace to put others first and to give ourselves up for them, whether it is in small ways or in big ways.

Amen.

- SATURDAY 31 -
Testify

To testify is to tell, to bear witness, to share, to offer, and to give. More specifically, it is to tell, to bear witness, to share, to offer, and to give out of our own lives because the only truths to which we can testify are those truths we have discovered in our own experiences.

To tell anything else may well be to tell the truth, but it is to tell a second-hand truth; it is not to testify.

O God, put and keep us in touch with our lives so that we might know the truth that is there.

O God, give us integrity that causes us to tell the same story with our words, with our actions, and even with our motivations.

O God, help us to testify to the truth of our relationship with you in ways that will bear witness to your grace, mercy, and love.

Amen.

- SATURDAY 32 -
Hallelujah

The biblical word "hallelujah" means "Praise the Lord"
—and that is something we should do every day.

Praise the Lord for the lives we live!
Praise the Lord for the air we breathe!
Praise the Lord for the water we drink!
Praise the Lord for the food we eat!
Praise the Lord for the people we love!
Praise the Lord for the homes we have!
Praise the Lord for the grace we know!
Praise the Lord for the love we share!
Praise the Lord for the fun we have!
Praise the Lord for the help we get!
Praise the Lord for the help we give!

Praise the Lord for the forgiveness we experience!
Praise the Lord for the suffering we endure!
Praise the Lord for the obstacles we overcome!
Praise the Lord for the victories we know!
Praise the Lord for the patience we learn!
Praise the Lord for the deaths we die!
Praise the Lord for the resurrection we experience!

Praise the Lord! Hallelujah!

Amen.

- SATURDAY 33 -

Lists

We have lists of things we need to do
—and we will get most of them done.

We have lists of things we want to do
—and we will get some of them done.

Lord, grant that our lists will be sources of inspiration to us rather than sources of frustration for us.

Help us to prioritize the items on our lists so that we might give the bulk of our time and energy to what is important. At the same time, help us to act on some of the items on our lists that are fun or frivolous or even foolish so that we might remember the wisdom of lightening up.

And grant that the items at the top of both of our lists will never change—that we will always put first acts of devotion, of love, grace, mercy, sharing, sacrifice, and service.

Amen.

- SATURDAY 34 -
Witness

On the one hand Jesus said, "Let your light shine before others, so that they may see your good works and give glory to your Father in heaven" (Matt. 5:16).

On the other hand—and in the same sermon, according to Matthew—he said, "Beware of practicing your piety before others in order to be seen by them; for then you have no reward from your Father in heaven" (Matt. 6:1).

So on the one hand Jesus tells us to do good works so that others can see them; on the other hand he tells us not to do them in order that we will be seen doing them.

The difference seems to be in the one to whom we want to bear witness: our Father in heaven or ourselves. Do we want what we do to draw attention to God or to us? Do we want people to say "So that's who God is" or to say, "My, what a fine person she/he is"?

O God, this is tough and we need a lot of help with it. It is so hard to stay on the right side of that line and even to know where the line is. After all, even if we think that our hearts really want you to be glorified, they may not. It is so easy for us to deflect to us praise intended for you.

So please help us, Lord. Guard our hearts. May our actions be of such a gracious quality that people who see them will catch a glimpse of who you are and be drawn to you. May our actions come from a heart that wants only to bear witness to you.

And if and as we grow toward that ideal, protect us from wanting to get credit for it.

Amen.

- SATURDAY 35 -
Quiet

Quiet is hard to come by in these days and in these lives. We are bombarded by noise and by words and by information to the extent that even when we shut off those sounds, we can't shut them off in our heads.

Teach us, Lord, to seek and to cultivate quiet. May your Spirit work with our minds to train us how to let go and to rest in the peace we have with you.

Still the chaos in our minds.
Calm the turmoil in our spirits.
Ease the burdens in our hearts.
Lessen the cacophony in our ears.

Cause us to love the quiet so that in it we can learn to hear your still small voice.

Then maybe we can hear it when the noise resumes.

Amen.

- SATURDAY 36 -
Place

Thank you, God, for the blessing of place.

Thank you for

a place to live,
a place to stand,
a place to love,
a place to rest,
a place to recover,
a place to belong—

a place to be.

In the midst of our restlessness, O God, cause us not to overlook the gift of place; lead us to accept it and to appreciate it and to enjoy it—even as we continue to search for it.

Bless those who truly have little or no sense of place; help them at least—and it is no small thing—to find and to know their place in you.

Amen.

- SATURDAY 37 -
Margins

Margins are the extra spaces on the edge of a sheet of writing paper marked off by light usually red borders that tell us "when writing don't go past here."

We do sometimes, though, and for various reasons.

Sometimes we get sloppy.
Sometimes we get inspired.
Sometimes we get careless.
Sometimes we get involved.
Sometimes we get tired.
Sometimes we get excited.

Sometimes whether we stay inside the lines or go outside them depends on whether anyone is going to check our work.

Lord, in our daily living, give us discernment to know when to stay inside the lines and when to go outside. Give us discernment to know, when we do go past the borders, whether we are doing so for good or bad reasons.

Some of our borders are there because you put them there, some because we put them there, some because others put them there.

Some of our margins constitute forbidden zones, some constitute extra available space, some constitute room for creativity and experimentation.

When we should stay within the lines, help us to do so with grace and discipline. When we should go over into the margins, help us to do so with courage and passion.

Amen.

- SATURDAY 38 -
Ellipsis

We use an ellipsis to indicate a place where words have been left out.

We may leave words out of a quotation in a paper because they are not pertinent to the point we are trying to make. In that case we are attempting to be prudent in our use of words, but we need to be careful lest we by omission change the meaning of the person we're quoting.

Lord, we have to leave words out in our hearing and in our speaking; our conversations and our memories are filled with ellipses. Help us not to leave out anything important; help us not to inappropriately change the meaning of our lives by what we leave out. At the same time, give us a healthy filter so that we might not cling to words that do neither us nor anyone else any good.

We may also use an ellipsis at the end of a sentence to indicate there is more to be said, but we choose not to say it. That's a very honest use of an ellipsis because there is always much more that could be said and because the future is always open.

Lord, we thank you for, even as we ask you to help us embrace, the incompleteness and possibilities and uncertainties and potential and mystery of our lives.

We will wait in trust and in hope.

Amen.

- SATURDAY 39 -
Sabbath

God commands us to take

a day to take off to take it as it comes,
a day to let up to let it happen,
a day to rest to let it rest.

Lord, forgive us for the conceit that causes us to live as if it is all up to us and to live as if we take off or let up or rest for one day a week it will all fall apart; it is a large conceit given that such holding of things together is your job, not ours.

Heal us of our workaholism and anxiety and franticness and fretting; we have for many years been scurrying along beside the Sabbath pool that contains the healing waters, but we have refused to get in.

Help us now to sit, to take up our chairs, and to rest in you.

Six days a week let us gladly tote our load and do what is ours to do.
One day a week let us gladly lay down our load and just be what is ours to be.

Amen.

- SATURDAY 40 -
Desire

It is possible to do all the right things but to be all the wrong ways; guard us from such a way of living, O Lord.

It is possible, for example, never to take someone or something that belongs to someone else, but at the same time to lust for a person or a possession to a degree that damages our spirits and impacts our relationships and negatively colors our entire approach to life.

Lord, we thank you for those characteristics that make us human, and we do not ask you to take them away from us. Asking that would be asking you to make us less than or more than human when what we really need to ask is that you would make us fully human, that you would make us all you intend for us to be and that you in Christ make it possible for us to be.

So we do not ask you to take away our desires, to take away our instinct to notice or to appreciate someone or something that is beautiful or good; indeed, we ask you to make us much more sensitive to the beauty and to the good in people and in objects so that we will not be captive to our culture's shallow view of what is beautiful and good.

At the same time, Lord, form in us an attitude toward and an approach to life and to the people and the things we encounter in life that will cause us to live in gratitude for who and what you have given and do and will give us, and for who and what you have and do and will give others.

Amen.

- SATURDAY 41 -
Gifts

Givers of true gifts give them with no expectation of reciprocation and with no creation of debt.

Recipients of true gifts receive them with no sense of deservingness and with no burden of repayment.

Give us grace, Lord, to be true givers of true gifts and true recipients of true gifts.

Help us freely to give and freely to receive.

May our only motivation in the ways we give or receive be a heart bursting with gratitude.

Amen.

- SATURDAY 42 -

Let Go

Sometimes we find ourselves holding on for dear life, in desperation clinging and grasping so that it doesn't all slip away.

We think in our fear and our pride that it is the strength and tenacity of our grip that will make the difference.

Forgive us, Lord.

Give us the grace and the trust instead to turn loose and to let go—to release it all to you.

It is better, after all, to slip or to fall or to collapse—even to die—in your arms than to hold on and to pull up—even to survive—by ours.

Remind us, Lord, that to hold on to our lives is to lose them while to let them go, to release them to you, is to gain them.

Amen.

- SATURDAY 43 -

Saints

We unfortunately tend sometimes to identify saints by what they are not: they are not liars or adulterers or thieves or gossips, or perhaps they are not practitioners of some behavior of which we disapprove.

We also unfortunately tend sometimes to evaluate our own sainthood by what we don't do or at least what we don't do in public. We are as good, we might believe, as we can cause other people to think we are.

Lord, forgive our shallowness and our silliness.

Help us to take note of and to emulate your true saints; help us to seek real sainthood—real holiness—and to live as real saints.

Help us to try hard enough, since it matters that it matters to us. But help us not to try too hard, since it is too easy for us to give ourselves too much credit for what only you can accomplish in us.

Help us to recall constantly that we are disciples of the only true and absolute saint who ever lived—and he had no place to lay his head, he was misunderstood and misjudged, he was despised and rejected, he was poor and outcast, and he suffered and died. Guard us, O Lord, from an unseemly attitude of triumphalism and sense of superiority.

Help us to be becoming holy from the inside out; grow our spirits so that Christ-like attitudes and feelings and motivations might empower and inform and inspire our actions.

Give us sanctity, O Lord, but protect us from sanctimony.

For all the saints, we thank you.
For our own sainthood, we trust you.

Amen.

- SATURDAY 44 -

Democracy

Democracy is government by the people.

That puts a lot of responsibility on the people;
sometimes we're up to it, and sometimes we aren't.

Forgive us, O God, when we shirk our responsibility.

Cause us, O God, to take our responsibility seriously.

Enlighten us, O God, so that we will see our responsibility to our nation as our responsibility to each other.

Help us, O God, even as we work toward being responsible for our democracy, to focus our ultimate trust on you and never on leaders—as sound as they may be—or on government—as constructive as it may be—or on a political party or platform or persuasion—as enticing as they may be.

Democracy is government by the people, so it cannot be wiser or nobler or kinder than the people. So make us wise, noble, and kind, O God.

Amen.

- SATURDAY 45 -

Them

There will always be the others; there will always be them. They are there. I notice them; I think of them; I act in relation to them.

Lord, when I notice them, let me notice their personhood and their humanity, not their category or their stereotype.

Lord, when I think of them, let me think of them as people who have abundant contributions to make and abundant needs to meet, not as people from whom I can get something or who want something from me.

Lord, when I act in relation to them, let me act for their good and in respect of their integrity, not for their harm or with manipulation for my purposes.

Lord, help me to remember that to those who are the others to me, I am one of the others to them.

Cause us to see each other, to think of each other, and to treat each other as we want to be seen, to be thought of, and to be treated.

Amen.

- SATURDAY 46 -
Reunions

Reunions are by definition events at which we get back together with people with whom we have not been for a while; there once was a "union," and now there will be a redo of the union—a "reunion."

Reunions are usually bittersweet. On the one hand it's good to see people again to whom we were once close; on the other hand we can hardly help but wonder why, since we were once so close and since we are so glad to see each other again, we didn't stay in closer touch or in touch at all—and whether we will now.

Reunions are also bittersweet because people to whom we were close are almost bound to have caused us at least one moment of deep joy and/or one moment of deep pain, whether they knew it or not and whether they remember it or not—but we know they did and we probably don't remember some of the ones we caused or inflicted, either.

Still, it's good to see them; still, we missed them; still, we will mean it when we say we will stay in touch with them—we really will.

Lord, thank you for reunions; thank you for the chance to catch up with each other, for the opportunity to share our lives again and to share the joys and the sorrows we all have known since we last saw each other; thank you for what we once were to each other; thank you for what we will be to each other, at least for a little while; thank you for what we may yet be to each other.

And Lord, thank you for that great reunion yet to come. It will be interesting to find out if the key to the experience will be what we can't forget or what we can't remember about each other.

Amen.

- SATURDAY 47 -
Stop

Some of us, on the one hand, stop too much.

We stop before we ever start and so accomplish nothing.
We stop too soon after we start and so accomplish little.
We stop too often working on what we started, so we seldom finish.

O God, deliver us from the fragmentation and frustration that result from the habit of stopping too much.

Some of us, on the other hand, don't stop enough.

We don't stop, even though stopping would give us a better perspective on what we're trying to accomplish.

We don't stop, even though stopping would give us an awareness that we're not indispensable and that the world goes on without our help.

We don't stop, even though stopping would give us some much-needed rest that would help us to be more human even as we're more productive.

O God, deliver us from the fragmentation and frustration that result from the habit of stopping too little.

Help us, O God, not to stop too much.
Help us, O God, not to stop too little.

Amen.

- SATURDAY 48 -
Finish

It is good to finish a job or a task or a project; thank you, Lord, for what we finish.

There is a sense, though, in which nothing is ever finished; more could be done to anything, and everything that is done is a piece of a larger picture that is certainly never completed.

So even as we celebrate what we finish, we ask for perspective and for grace that will enable us to live with and even thrive in this perpetually unfinished universe of yours.

After all, O Lord, one day we will be finished here—but we will just be getting started.

Amen.

- SATURDAY 49 -
Forever

Forever is a long time.
This moment is the beginning of forever.

Forever is important.
This moment is important.

Lord, keep me constantly filled with the realization that this present moment is a part of forever and thus should be given the same weight I give to my anticipated everlasting future.

Perhaps I can't live as freely and fully now as I will when I live outside of time in eternity, but surely your eternal life in me now means I can live much more freely and fully in this moment than I am doing.

Let it be, dear Lord.

Amen.

- SATURDAY 50 -
Emmanuel

It's a Hebrew word that means "God with us."
Thank God that God is indeed with us.

Thank you, God, for being with us in the natural world;
we sense your presence in the wonder of your creation.

Thank you, God, for being with us in each other; we sense your presence in the love we find in human community.

Thank you, God, for being with us in Jesus Christ; we sense your presence in our encounters with the living Christ in the Gospel stories and in our encounters with the risen Christ in our stories.

Thank you, God, for being with us in the Holy Spirit; we sense your presence in our lives through the communion we have day in and day out with your Spirit.

Compel and inspire us every day to live in light of the fact of your presence with us, O God.

Amen.

- SATURDAY 51 (OR CHRISTMAS DAY) -
Nativity

Christ the Savior is born

in Bethlehem,
in the world,
in time,
in space,
in me,
in you,
in us,
in them,
in perpetuity.

Christ the Savior is born.

And as it was in the beginning, is now, and ever shall be…
…so we thank you, O God.

Amen.

- SATURDAY 52 -

Back

As I look back,

teach me to evaluate what is over and done with,
not with wistfulness but rather with wisdom;

teach me to acknowledge failures,
not with regret but rather with repentance;

teach me to celebrate accomplishments,
not with pride but with praise.

Amen.

CPSIA information can be obtained at www.ICGtesting.com
Printed in the USA
LVOW130802070612

285012LV00004B/1/P